From Matzah Balls *to* My Bible

MY JOURNEY TO FINDING GOD

HEIDI CLARKE

ISBN 978-1-68517-115-5 (paperback)
ISBN 978-1-68517-116-2 (digital)

Christian Faith Publishing
832 Park Avenue
Meadville, PA 16335
www.christianfaithpublishing.com

Printed in the United States of America

In loving memory of my friend Colleen who is gone yet will never be forgotten. Your spirit will live on forever in our hearts, and may we all experience the peace of your absence here on earth through God's beautiful sunsets on Keuka Lake.

Psalm 73:26
> "My flesh and my heart may fail, but God is the strength of my heart and my portion forever."

To my children, Chandler, Emma and Noah. May you all have your own journey to share one day about how you found God. And to my husband who encouraged me to simply do what I love and what was important to me.

Contents

Preface

I have chosen to write this book for the sake of sharing *my* story. Everyone has their own story of things that shape their lives, and I felt convicted in many ways to share mine because it is a story that maybe someone will relate to. And in relating to my story, you may be able to rewrite your own. Without having found God, my story would likely have had a very different outcome filled with nothing really positive. I would not have had the courage in many situations along the way without having had the love and strength that can only come from a relationship with God. As you read my story, it is my hope that you can begin to see the transformation of a life with God and a life without God. It has not been easy and has required a lot of work and commitment on my part. I often equate how hard it can be with the notion of exercise. Everyone wants a healthy, fit body, but if you don't put in the work, you likely won't have one. Everyone's path may look a little different, but my hope is you will choose to seek Him in a way that is meaningful for you.

May the power of the Holy Spirit help me to find the words needed to convey my message. I leave you now with a piece of scripture that has resonated with me from the beginning. It is from the book of Isaiah chapter 41 verses 9 to 10. I will share it first from the New International Version (NIV) and second from the message.

> I took you from the ends of the earth, from its farthest corners I called you. I said, 'You are my servant'; I have chosen you and have not rejected you. So do not fear, for I am with you; do not be dismayed, for I am your God. I will

strengthen you and help you; I will uphold you with my righteous right hand.

I pulled you in from all over the world, called you in from every dark corner of the earth, Telling you, 'You're my servant, serving on my side. I've picked you. I haven't dropped you.' Don't panic. I'm with you. There's no need to fear for I'm your God. I'll give you strength. I'll help you. I'll hold you steady, keep a firm grip on you.

My Prayer

Father, *thank you* never seems to be enough. You have provided for me, protected me, and given me strength when I have felt weak and beaten down. Father, I pray that I can share my story in a way that will help others to want to grow to know you. I pray that you will help me to find the words needed to tell this story so that others may be inspired and your name glorified. I am forever yours, Father, and will continue to share your truths just as you commanded me to. Thank you. I pray these things in your precious name. Amen.

Acknowledgments

There are many people along the way who have helped me take this journey, and without them, I may still be worrying about whether or not I made my matzah ball soup. Thank you to Kelly for introducing me to my Bible and God. Without your friendship and support in understanding the process, I likely wouldn't be here writing about this journey. You have a beautiful gift of sharing the word of God, and this journey began because of a Facebook post you made about a ladies' group. It has been seven years since that post in September of 2014, and along the way, I have not only grown in God's word. But I have learned so much about the meaning of true friendship from the many women who joined our special Bible study every Tuesday morning. We were all just a group of women seeking God so that we could become better wives, mothers, sisters, and friends. We were all in search of a place where others could support us through the ups and downs of life using the truth so beautifully written in the Bible. Thank you, Kelly, for leading us all to that special Tuesday morning, for that is truly where the best part of my journey has begun.

∞

Chapter 1

FROM THE BEGINNING

"Dig deep and begin with what it was like growing up—really say it like it is!" This was my reminder from my husband as I wrote.

"Heidi, did you make your matzah ball soup?" These were the words I would hear every April during the Jewish holiday of Passover. I was led to believe my whole life that being a Jew was really special. We were a special group of people who shared special traditions; and oftentimes, I got the sense that we were maybe better than others. So if this was true, then why did I feel like something was missing in my life? Why did I feel like I really didn't have a sense of who I was like deep inside? I have memories of being a really happy, smiley little girl with a big personality. But as I got older, that longing for who I really was felt like an empty space in my soul.

As a child, the old films showed a dirty blond-haired, little girl who was always looking to be the center of attention in the movie. I apparently loved to dance and sing, and pictures of me seemed to always show a girl who appeared to be really happy. I guess you could say, the old movies and pictures reflect what Facebook is today. Everyone's life looks great in pictures, but pictures don't always reveal the truth behind them. How I felt on the inside was not the same as how I appeared on the outside. Inside, I lacked confidence big time, always felt others were luckier than me, smarter than me, prettier than me; and the list goes on and on. I can remember wanting so badly to be liked by others. I would do what I could to try and fit in. I guess you could say I was a follower at times. If a group of girls were being mean to another girl, I would go along with it just to be accepted and to fit in. I believe people sometimes have an escape from the reality they are immersed in. My sister was a reader, and books probably took her out of her reality. I believe my escape was doing the things that got me positive attention. Singing enabled me to receive compliments from others around me. Performing was a way of being someone I didn't really feel I was on the inside. I became a different person when I performed, and that person seemed to be the one others liked. I also spent a lot of time at friends' houses because, at my friends' homes, I seemed to be accepted for who I was. For one thing, I was always welcomed by their parents with a sense of them being glad I was there. I had great manners, which I credit my mom with. She was a stickler about being polite and that I was. I had the *thank you*s and *please*s down pat, and I always knew to find the parent and say goodbye and thank you before leaving. However, at my house, life was not always so jolly. My mom always seemed mad about something. If I wanted to have friends over, she was annoyed. If I took a snack, she was annoyed that I messed up her kitchen. It was like you could never do anything right in her eyes. There was always constant criticism, and it was always directed in a way that left you feeling terrible and guilty. Reflecting on this person that I described earlier, you can see how a pattern develops when someone is taught to believe they will never measure up. My sister was super smart, and she was criticized for always reading. I was super social, and I was criticized for liking friends more than my family. Accepting us for who we were just didn't seem to be the way it was. It's hard to even put this to paper, but I can remember being called dumb by members of my family many times. In fact, my mother always had a calendar that the library would send out. She once told me that my birthday fell on national ding-a-ling day and that it was on the library calendar. I believed it and even, in later life, googled it to see if it actually existed. Your guess is right, it did not. My mother was just a mean person who, I believe, said mean things to help herself feel better about who she was. I would bet anything that my mother was verbally abused as a child and, instead of trying to break the cycle of being a person who does that, my mother just continued it.

Breaking the cycle of how you were raised and doing better is hard. Facing your true self, your strengths, and weaknesses is never easy. As you see, I had to do that, and I began to do that in counseling. It wasn't until years later that I would learn how to fight these demons using the word of God. It is a daily challenge but one I have committed to and one I will continue to use for the rest of my life. Putting on the armor of God is the only defense we have against the evil that is presented in our lives. I will continue to fight for my inner freedom and to live the life that God intended for me. I will seek, study, question, pray, and be a disciple to others as best I can. If God can touch my life, He can touch yours too.

I have started and stopped the writing of this book a multitude of times. It seems that every time I go to write, I worry about what my family would think if they read this. You see, in the world I grew up in, you were predestined to be someone that your parents saw you to be. That someone is not who I turned out to be. In fact, I went against the grain on all levels, beginning with questioning my faith.

I am not a writer! I mean, I love writing; and oftentimes, I will reread journal entries from devotions I read or just excerpts of things I write about my faith and think, *Wow did I write that?* Writing has sort of become a lost art; but I love writing cards, and I love writing my thoughts. However, a book is not an undertaking I ever thought I would do or felt qualified to do. But the more I listen to my soul, the louder God's voice appears to me. It's like He is telling me that my story is important, and it needs to be told. I want to honor God in any way I can. So I'm going to give this writing thing a try, and I hope my writing will touch one person who may have the same questions I have had about finding God and understanding that faith evolves and is a process. I love that idea because it allows me to not feel stuck. It helps me to be grounded, in that I know Jesus loves me and is always there. But He is changing me, and with that change comes wisdom, questions, and thoughts. So this is my attempt at putting this altogether in some organized fashion so that you can hear my story and be inspired by it. Hopefully, you will be encouraged as well to seek answers to questions you may have. Finding your place in life is a journey; and I'm so glad you are along for the ride.

It wasn't until just a few years ago that I met God and was able to navigate how developing a relationship with him would help me become the person I am today. The person I am today knows how to wear the armor of God to fight the demons in my life. Some days are harder than others to do so, and that is also a part of this journey we go on when we try to grow in our faith. So much of who we are or who we become as people is influenced by the way we are raised and how we are treated by those around us. I will share my story, but I want to make it clear that it has taken years for me to remove the bitterness about how my upbringing impacted the person I was, and how I am now able to recognize that the most important thing in life is to know that you are God's child first and loved by Him.

Learning about who God is, is not something that was taught to me through my Jewish upbringing. As I recall events in my life related to my Jewish upbringing, it became clear that Judaism was more a religion of tradition in how we practiced as a family. There was also a definite feeling that I should be proud to be a Jew, yet I never really understood why. However, what makes Jewish people special, I learned about on my journey to find God.

I was raised as a typical Jewish girl on Long Island. I went to a Hebrew school, was a bat mitzvah on November 14, 1982, grew up in a predominantly Jewish neighborhood, and was told that I was not allowed to date someone who wasn't Jewish. My family was very typical of other Jewish families we knew. We attended temple on Rosh Hashanah, the Jewish New Year, and Yom Kippur, a Day of Atonement and a day of fasting. It was a big deal each year to get a new outfit to wear to temple as it sometimes seemed more like a fashion show than a place of worship. I went to a conservative temple, not because we were law-abiding Jews but because the temple was conveniently located across the street in walking distance.

My memories of attending synagogue do not really reflect ones of deep worship. Most of what I remember was sitting in the bathroom with my friends while our parents sat in the synagogue, listening to the cantor sing songs and pray in Hebrew alongside the rabbi. If I recall, there was a loudspeaker in the bathroom so you could hear what was taking place in the synagogue. But if I joined my parents, it was always with the notion that I would get out before the rabbi's sermon. If you did not get out before that, you were "stuck" in the service until the sermon was finished, which was usually an hour. To be honest, I have no recollection of any message from any sermon I ever got "stuck" in. What I do remember was people talking and whispering while the rabbi spoke, and oftentimes, the rabbi would have to ask the congregation to be quiet. After temple, we would come home, get out of our uncomfortable clothes, eat a meal as a family, and that was it. Nothing was ever mentioned about the sermon or the biblical lesson learned.

On Rosh Hashanah, we usually had my mom's pot roast with these little white potatoes from a can baked with some paprika on them, challah bread, and my mom's noodle pudding, which was basically egg noodles baked into a casserole using egg as a binder, lots of cinnamon, yellow raisins, and apples. Noodle pudding was the one dish everyone always seemed to like. I can recall at dinner, my mom would commend herself that the noodle pudding wasn't dry, yet she made it as if cooking this dinner was the most dreadful task. I never helped or even thought to help because my mother never wanted anyone in *her* kitchen. Let me fast-forward to a funny story about my "mom's kitchen." I can remember one time when I was a freshman in college; it was winter break, and I was rushed to the hospital in severe pain. I remember being in my bed in excruciating pain and being afraid to go into my parents' room to tell them I needed to go to the emergency room. I was afraid that my mother would be mad and would yell at me, but I had no choice. I recall being alone in the back seat of the car, screaming in pain, and my mother yelling at me that it was probably from all the drinking I did at college. After some testing, we learned I had a kidney stone, which is probably one of the worst pains someone can have. At any rate, while I was in the hospital, my sister and brother excitedly baked me a cake for my birthday. As expected, my mother went off the handle. She was so mad at them for doing this because they probably made a mess in *her* kitchen. Could you even imagine being mad at your children for doing something of this nature? But this was how things were at our house. I think it almost became normal.

Yom Kippur was the other holiday we went to temple for. It is a day you are supposed to atone your sins by fasting and spending the daytime in prayer. However, what I remember most about Yom Kippur was everyone talking about how hungry they were and asking when we were going to break fast. My mom always prepped the food ahead of time, which she would leave in the refrigerator so that at sundown, the food would all be ready for devouring. Because you fasted from sundown the night before to sundown on the day of Yom Kippur, you never ate heavy stuff for your meal. We would have bagels, lox and cream cheese, whitefish salad, egg salad, tuna salad, pickled herring, more noodle pudding, and my dad would always have some type of boxed Danish that no one liked but him. Every year he would say, "Come on, Heidi, have a piece of Danish. It's good." And every year I would say, "Dad, I don't like Danish."

Although I do not have a lot of memories of feeling any connection to God while attending temple, I did also attend temple three days a week for quite a few years. You see, I attended Hebrew school every Tuesday and Thursday from 4:00 to 6:00 p.m. and every Sunday morning from 9:00 to 11:00 a.m. I do remember one class in Hebrew school where we sang. And because singing was something I loved, I remember liking that class and being somewhat happy to be there. We sang everything in Hebrew; and so I have no idea what I was singing about. But I got to sing nonetheless, and I loved that. There was another class we took, which I believe talked about the historical side of things. But what I remember most about the class was one student who was one of those smart-ass kids who would always challenge the teacher. It was always funny to hear what would come out of his mouth and how he and the teacher would argue, eventually leading to him being kicked out. We also had a class where we learned the Hebrew letters and some basic words, like mother, father, table, and chair. I liked that class too because I always enjoyed any class that involved language. I can still read some Hebrew as long as there are vowels. So that's it. That is my Jewish education in a nutshell. One must wonder, why would you go through all of this? And the answer of course is to have a bat mitzvah.

It is tradition and common practice that when a Jewish girl turns twelve, they enter into religious maturity. However, many are thirteen and even close to fourteen by the time they may have a bat mitzvah. Bat mitzvah is Hebrew for "daughter of commandment." At that time, a girl takes on the rights and obligations of a Jewish adult, which include the commandments of the Torah. She is supposed to, from that day forward, observe mitzvot, which includes things such as lighting the Shabbat candles, fasting on Yom Kippur, and performing acts of charity. Although many Jews do not observe mitzvot, it is the notion that once you go through a mitzvah, you are encouraged to take part in the religious and spiritual experiences. I am no expert on all of this; therefore, I am not going to try and explain it all because the bottom line for me is that all of this did not help me to develop my relationship with God. In fact, I still didn't know who God was.

Having a bat mitzvah, from what I recall, was about a party. I got to invite like sixty friends or more to a country club where we had a DJ, a photographer who captured the night, party favors, good food, and drinks for the adults. It was so much fun especially because I got to be the star of the party! I sat in a big wicker chair at the head of the table, and late in the night, they wheeled in Heidi's candy store where everyone got to take treats from cotton candy to candy apples. It was a ton of fun, and I really appreciated the party that was thrown for me. But as I look back, I feel as though this whole experience was about the party. As a reminder, I am not here to tell anyone else's story but my own. Other Jewish children may have had a totally different experience than mine, but I am here to share my journey to finding God, which is what was missing from my life for so many years.

It was fun growing up in a predominantly Jewish neighborhood because I got to experience really fun bar and bat mitzvahs. Every weekend, it seemed as though I had another big party to go to. And because I grew up in Long Island, some of the parties were in New York City at night clubs. It really was a ton of fun; but no one, to my knowledge, ever spoke about the spiritual part of being a mitzvah. We all talked a lot about the party, but God and faith were two words that were missing both in conversations with other kids who were bar and bat mitzvahed; yet more importantly, they were missing in my life. The deep desire for something more was there, but I just didn't know what it was that was missing. However, after reflecting on my upbringing, it is clear that it was a deep sense of spirituality that was missing. Because I didn't have anyone in my social circle who talked about faith or God, I had no way of navigating what this really was.

My family, although very supportive financially, really did not play any role in developing my search for what was missing. I often thought the reason I didn't connect with my family was because I was a very deep person who focused a lot on emotional intelligence. Anytime I tried to talk from a place of feelings, I was told by my mom to "stop the psychoanalytical bullshit." I now believe that God had a plan for my life. And sometimes, seeking God on your own teaches you the most. I have many friends today who were raised Christians—some Catholics, some Lutherans, some Presbyterians, and the list goes on. I also have friends who do not identify with any Christian denomination, and so they are called nondenominational Christians. No matter how my friends were raised, almost all of them have shared with me that seeking on their own is what has strengthened their relationship with God. Sharing the truths so eloquently written in the Bible with other women truly helps you to grow, and I just feel so blessed that I was led to this ladies' group, for that really kick-started my journey!

Chapter 2

WHO I WAS

Growing up, I defined myself as a Jew, not because I connected in any way with what it meant to be Jewish but that is what my bloodline was. Jewish traditions were passed down, and I never really questioned it because I wanted to do the right thing according to how my parents saw things. There was one family in our cul-des-ac who was not Jewish; but pretty much, most of the people I associated with were. However, I continued to feel like I was missing something but couldn't put my finger on what it was. I felt this void, and with this void came a feeling of being unloved and just not good enough. I tried hard to fill that void, thinking that things or people would fulfill me. What I came to find out is more than I could have ever imagined.

Being Jewish to me was something I was unable to really hold an intelligent conversation about. I knew what I was told about being Jewish, and I never really questioned what it meant. I was born a Jew, and that obviously meant that I would be a Jew forever. However, being Jewish and having faith was not a connection that was ever made for me. Being Jewish meant honoring the traditions, and I personally did not recognize that God was a part of any of them. Having faith requires understanding the role God plays in your life. If you don't know God, then how do you have faith? In fact, faith was not even a word I believe I ever used. I was Jewish, not faithful. This was the question I began to seek unknowingly. When I say unknowingly, I mean because it wasn't until years later that the pieces of the puzzle started to make sense to me.

As I went through school, I obviously became interested in boys, and I remember the one rule my parents had: I was allowed to date boys, but only if the boy was Jewish. At the time, I didn't really question it, *for that was their wish.* Please note this statement as it plays out to be a powerful one in which I believe held me captive for many years. And to this day, it is something I have to be mindful of. However, there were times where I would wonder if there was something not good enough about non-Jews, but I came to my own conclusion that it was merely that they wanted to keep the Jewish religion going; and dating a non-Jew might interfere with that. Now of course, I met boys who were not Jewish, so I dated them and just told my parents they were half Jewish. In other words, I lied because I chose boys based on who they were as people, not what they were; and so for me that rule seemed really unfair. Something I always found bothersome was that my parents always seemed to form an opinion about others especially if a person's thinking did not align with theirs. I can remember numerous times questioning why my parents seemed to have an issue with many people. I guess you can say that it was acceptable to pass judgment on others. I loved people, learning about people, and really embraced how each of us was made differently. Remember, we were not religious Jews attending temple every Saturday morning for Shabbat service and celebrating holidays like Purim. We were the "good Jews" who made their matzah ball soup and had their children attend Hebrew school because that was just what you did to show you were a "good" Jew.

Growing up, I was the middle child. My sister was super smart; and my younger brother—well he was the golden boy they longed for. I was pegged as the pretty one, outgoing, and not very smart. School was hard for me. I hated to read, and I'd much rather be out with my friends than doing schoolwork. However, I tried hard and had a lot of tutors in math along the way. My family was an interesting dynamic to say the least. I mean, we were normal in what we looked like, but behind the closed door, that was where it became interesting.

My father worked very hard, six days a week; and my mom was a stay-at-home mom. My passion was singing and dancing. You could catch me on many occasions in my bedroom with my cassette recorder playing and me singing in the mirror, usually using my hair-brush as a microphone. When we would have any company over, I would stand on the hearth and entertain everyone by singing. I think the most memorable moment for me was in elementary school when I got to sing the solo of "Somewhere Over the Rainbow" during a concert. I can remember it vividly. I began the solo on stage wearing this beautiful yellow dress, and I got to walk down the center row of the gymnasium where chairs were on either side. I held a micro-phone, and I just felt like a superstar. I don't really recall my family making a big deal about any of my performances. In fact, sometimes it felt as though I celebrated these accomplishments on my own. When I would sing in my room for endless hours, I would be made fun of and mocked. It was sort of the same for my sister from what I remember. She spent a lot of time reading, and my mom often made fun of her for that. But her reading is what led to her future accomplishments in life. Encouragement was something that was obsolete in my life growing up. Instead of being lifted up about who I was, I was made to feel badly about who I was and was constantly compared to others as well as my sister. However, that never made sense to me because they mocked her for being smart too. As my husband puts it today, you just could never have done anything right. The sad part about this is the long-lasting ramifications it can have on an individual. How do you feel worthy for who you are when the people who are supposed to love you the most make fun of you? This is where finding God can help. Unfortunately, I still didn't know this at the time, and so my life went on; and I really didn't know any difference, nor did I really reflect on how this made me feel. You become accustomed to the situations in your life; and sometimes at a young age, you fail to question things because you believe your parents do everything right. Fast-forwarding a bit here and where I am today in my beliefs and relationship with God, it is clear that

He feels I'm worthy. It was His voice which has led me to wanting to share my story. In fact, I don't want to share it, but I feel led to. There is a difference in that. I have learned that it is important to do what God leads you to do. We all hear His voice differently, and this is something that I didn't realize for some time. However, it is clear to me now that many of my issues with lack of confidence actually stem from how I was raised, for I believe confidence can grow when it's nurtured by your family and those closest to you. Confidence can also come from the love God has for you as His child. But when you don't know God, you can't use Him to guide your path in life. Instead, you lean on the guidance of your parents; and unfortunately, this landed me in a ditch, so to speak. My life truly played out in a way that left me feeling not very good about myself. I was able to put on a front because performing was something I loved to do; however, you can pretend to be someone you are not or someone you want to be, but in the quiet, the pain of how I really felt about myself always lingered inside. This void eventually became a curse because I sought love in all the wrong ways with relationships. It wasn't until my adult life that I can look back and reflect on this and say to myself, *If I had only known then what I know now.* My faith has brought me to a place I never dreamed of getting, but that story will unfold as I continue to write.

I moved on with my singing, and I can remember another great event in my life. It was in junior high, and we had blue-and-gold day for spirit week. We had a talent competition in the gymnasium, and I sang "Tomorrow" from the show *Annie*. The lyrics were "the sun'll come out tomorrow…" I remember sitting on the piano while someone played the music, and I can vividly recall the applause and feeling really happy about my performance. I don't remember if we won or if I was even blue or gold, but I do remember the moment and the feeling I had of pure elation. This was another moment in my life where I believe God was speaking to me. The light of the sun would shine for me, but it was going to take some time for me to see it and eventually be led by it.

I took drama in high school and got parts in plays along the way, but my passion was really in singing more than acting. I loved everything about performing, yet I never really pursued it. It's funny because now that I am a parent and have children of my own, I hop on any passion my children may display, and I encourage them as best I can. I think I lacked that from my family growing up; and oftentimes, I guess, when you are not encouraged to do something, you begin to think maybe you are not so good at the thing you are doing, and you then lose the drive to do it at all. No blame here, just honesty. We as parents do the best we can; and I believe in my heart, that's what my parents did. We often navigate life based on how we ourselves were parented; but when you allow God to be a part of your life, you enter a path that is filled with truth and love. The truth here is that I was an incredible person and loved by God. But again, not knowing God impacted who I believed I was, and it was based on false perceptions that were presented by those who were supposed to love me most—my family.

During my senior year, my mom woke up one morning with what we thought at the time was Bell's palsy. That is when half your face becomes paralyzed, and you don't have movement on that side of your face. After many tests and appointments, my mom was diagnosed with multiple sclerosis. It was a shocking diagnosis. I remember one afternoon, watching my dad leave the house and go into the backyard and repeatedly hit a tree with a stick all the while with tears streaming down his face. As Jews, one would think that maybe turning to the rabbi would be the next step for seeking some counsel; but nope, there was none of that. My mother continued on, and her attitude in life became even more negative. She was mad at the world, so to speak. Unfortunately for her, she did not have a relationship with God, so her anger ate away at her; and in turn, this anger was directed toward all of us. This is important to note because the way our parents handle difficult situations often becomes the blueprint for our life and how we handle tough situations. Not once did my family ever talk about calling upon God for strength or even the Jewish religion. Life really became a series of events that you yourself would go through, and I was learning that there was no faith or goodness in horrible situations. I recall her one time, out of anger, saying, "I hope you get MS someday!" Can you even imagine saying that to your child, wishing ill on them because of how unhappy you are with your own situation? Most parents would trade positions with their children if their children were ill, and I had a mother who was wishing it upon me because of how far removed she was in her faith. Someone who knows God and the Lord Jesus Christ would never say these words or harbor those feelings. Satan was having a field day with my mother. She had no weapons against the evilness lurking around her. Today, I am not angry about this. At the time, I was; but now I realize that she didn't know any better because she never chose to seek beyond being a good Jew who made her matzah ball soup. Again, there are plenty of wonderful Jewish people. This is not a bash on the religion of Judaism. This is my story of how being Jewish was not enough.

Off to college, I went in 1985. I attended Ithaca College in what people downstate consider to be upstate NY. In college, you really broaden your horizons because when you grow up in one area your whole life, you think that's what life is like everywhere. Boy, was I wrong! There was so much more out there than I ever knew. I experienced camping for the first time, boating on freshwater lakes, tubing, waterskiing, hiking gorges, and really experiencing the outdoors more than I ever had. Maybe this was God speaking to me, beginning to introduce me to Him. Like He was saying to me, "Heidi, look at the beauty around you and appreciate it, for I created it all!" However, I really wasn't thinking that at the time. I was merely trying to get through courses, meet new people, and have fun! In fact, one of my best friends I met in my freshman year told me that she was from Rome, and I remember saying, "You are from Rome, Italy?" Again, I had never heard of another Rome before, but she was talking about Rome, New York. I was so sheltered in how I grew up. The only thing I knew about not being Jewish was the Italian family who lived across the cul-de-sac from us. I knew they weren't Jewish because they celebrated holidays that we didn't. That was what I knew about people who were not Jewish. I had no idea there was so much more to it. However, I loved having friends like my friend Donna because I got to experience Christian holidays like Easter for the first time. I had no concept as to what Easter really was, but we ate a lot of amazing Italian food. And after living on a college diet, it was really pretty awesome when someone made homemade pizza for your snack! At any rate, my eyes began to open at college, and I think I began to see things in a way I hadn't up to this point. However, it has only been since I have reflected on all of this that I can now see the whole picture and how God's hand was in this from the beginning.

College was an interesting experience for me. You see, I had gone away to school with a boyfriend, and that became problem number one for me. Once I realized there was a whole world out there, I was pretty sure having a boyfriend was probably not going to be the best way to go through college. Unfortunately for me, my boyfriend didn't see it that way. He was four years older than me, and I really hadn't yet grown as an independent person. Four years was a big difference at this young age. When I finally ended it, he drove up from Long Island and showed up at my dorm room. He called and harassed me and told me horrible things about myself that I actually believed to be true. There was that lack of confidence in myself creeping in again.

Love in my family was something you did not talk about. My parents never told me they loved me, and so I never returned the words back to them. I'm not sure I really knew what love was. Love and God were two words I don't remember ever being used in my home. Remember, I was told basically that I was a ding-a-ling as my mother claimed it was a holiday on the calendar. This is just another reason as to why it is so important to know God because, ultimately, He is your Father and loves you and thinks the world of you. God provides you with hope; and without God in your life, there is no hope. However, the funny thing about who I was is that other people really seemed to love me. My friends' moms always chatted with me, and I always seemed to have such wonderful relationships with them. I spent a lot of time with one friend through the early years of high school, and I loved her family. Her parents were such loving people, and they extended that love to me. To this day, her family is still a beautiful sight I get to see on Facebook. I was fortunate to travel on vacation with them, and it helped me to see what love looks like and how a family can be loving, get along, and have fun. The memories I have of my family vacations was my mother yelling about preparing to pack and just always finding ways to be unhappy even in the happiest times. One moment that stands out to me, because again it was a moment I was made to feel dumb, was when we were on vacation in California. I had asked what time we were going to eat dinner, and my mom said 5:30–6:00. And I said, "5:36, why not 5:35?" I guess one might laugh at it and move on, but I became defined by that comment as the dumb one and continued to be reminded of it for years to come. In the later part of high school, I had another friend I grew close to, and her mom was like a mom to me as well. I guess you can say I had surrogate moms growing up; but truthfully, no one can really take the place of your own mom. While growing up, I wasn't really paying attention to the fact that I was possibly learning what a close relationship looked like between a daughter and a mom. But now looking back, I recognize that God put those moms in my life for a reason.

My mom was not a fan of me having friends at our house. If I mentioned it, I would hear, "I just mopped the floors." Funny because I mop mine now usually with kids and dogs scurrying through the wet floor to get to where they need to go. At any rate, I had a lot of friends and tried very hard not to be home a lot of the time. However, that was not an easy thing to do as my parents would chastise me about why I needed to sleep out or why I was always doing something. They would say, "Can't you ever stay home?" My thought was, *Why would I want to do that? It wasn't like we were a fun family who gathered together to play a game or sit and talk and laugh or a family who shared what was going on in our lives with each other.* I can vividly remember being in sixth grade, and on Fridays, everyone would be making their plans for the weekend. I would be asked if I wanted to sleep over at a friend's house, and I would become so anxious because I would want to so badly, but I knew that meant I had to ask, and I knew my mom's immediate response would be an angry no. Sometimes after begging and pleading, she would drive me, but my night was usually ruined by then because I was worrying that my mom was mad at me and that affected me having a good time.

Sunday mornings are pretty memorable for me. Before we would leave for Hebrew school, I would usually be eating my bowl of cereal alongside my sister and brother eating theirs. My dad, being that it was his one day off, would ask my mom to make pancakes or eggs, something I guess a little special since it was the only morning he was not off to work, scoffing a bowl of cereal down. I always remember my mom making the biggest deal out of this. She would get so mad, and my parents would be arguing, and it often ended with my mom "crying over the eggs." It sort of became a joke on Sunday. We would all wonder if "mom was going to cry over the eggs." She would get so angry at us that, on one occasion, I can remember her turning and yelling, "Fuck all of you!" At that point, leaving for Hebrew school was a welcoming thing. I felt like when I walked into the building, I had a sense of relief because things were always tense at home. It literally at times felt like an escape. However, I never connected that feeling to God. It was more a feeling like, "Yay, I get to see my friends!" It's sort of funny because, for the longest time, I thought maybe making pancakes was really hard. However, I remember the first time I made them from the box like my mom did, and it was super simple. To this day, I still wonder what the big deal was. Again, we all have the opportunity to see life through a different lens, and the lens my mom saw life through was not how I wanted to see it. God helped make it clear to me that my lens was going to change, but I still didn't know it.

My mental state after the breakup in freshman year was not good. I was extremely fragile, but I never talked to anyone about it but my friends. My friends were super supportive, and I felt their love. But still at this point, my parents seemed to brush off the issue and were more annoyed by my mental situation than anything. In fact, I feared calling my parents because we never seemed to discuss our feelings. I was just blamed for having any that were different from theirs. I never received counseling. And when I look back at this time in my life, I do see that I had a strength I wasn't even aware of. I had to face the shame of my mental instability yet still had to study for finals which I got through just fine. This for sure would be one of those moments where you would cry out to God, but I didn't know who God was; I was just crying out and hoping someone would make things right.

After Christmas break, life at college went back to normal. I definitely struggled figuring out who I was, and I officially told the boyfriend to leave me alone. I continued to date boys and seek that special feeling of love that was so lacking in my life. At this point, I just wanted to have fun with my friends and forget the whole boyfriend thing so that I could work on myself, except that I really didn't know what that meant. There were boys along the way, and one was kind of a longer relationship. But when that one ended, I told myself, "I am done dating for a while, and I'm just going to have fun." God had a different plan, and I believe to this day, my life took a different path; and without this path, I might be someone who repeated life the way my parents taught me to live it. For me, that would have led to a disaster.

It was now junior year, and my sociology classes were becoming super interesting. I loved my one professor who also happened to be my advisor, and I worked with her a lot outside of classes. As a result, I became a TA, or better known as a teacher's assistant, for one of her classes called mental health issues. Luckily for me, I got to do this with a close friend who I actually had gone to high school with. She and I had just returned from Christmas break and a vacation in Florida. It was now the start of our spring semester, and I remember walking into the class wearing a denim mini skirt, boots, and a black hat. I was tan and feeling on top of the world in my new role as TA. This was a lecture hall class, so there were quite a few students in the class. At the start of it, the students had to count off one to five so that they could be placed in a group with a set of TAs. I believe we were TA group two. Apparently, not to my knowledge at the time, one of the guys in the class was asked by another student to switch groups with him because he wanted to be in the group with his friend. God apparently had big plans here because that allowed this guy, Todd, to be in my group. We eventually met in our small groups, and I remember thinking that this guy, Todd, in our group was so cute. I came to find out later that he ended up in my group by chance. Well we can call it chance or the work of God. I truly believe this to be the start of God's plan for the rest of my life. Fast-forward to now, and this guy, Todd, became my husband. It was kinda funny to have met your husband in a class called mental health issues. We laugh about it to this day.

I really had thought I was done dating at Ithaca as I had just gotten out of a relationship a few months prior, and I was so over the boyfriend thing; but for some reason, I was drawn to Todd. He seemed to ask a lot of questions about me and genuinely took an interest in who I was. After countless conversations, one may have concluded that we came from two different worlds. But I was interested in his, and he in mine. We ended up becoming an item fairly quickly regardless of the fact that he was not Jewish and was raised in a Christian home having attended a Presbyterian Church. For some reason, I didn't even flinch at the idea of dating someone who wasn't Jewish even though I was well aware of the rule: no dating non-Jewish guys. In my gut, I just felt this was right and felt like he was a good person, and my parents would see that. My gut seems to be directly linked to decisions I am faced with in my life. Therefore, looking back, I believe that feeling in my gut was also God's way of making His presence known.

Todd could not be more different than me. He was not Jewish and from a really small town, south of Rochester, New York called Honeoye Falls. I know, you are all trying to figure out how to say it. Think of the expression "oy vey," and it's kind of like that. He didn't drive a fancy foreign car. In fact, my friend and I followed him to "S" lot, better known as "shit lot," at Ithaca one day after class. The key was to know what kind of car a guy drove so you could figure out if they were out at the bars. Well to my surprise, Todd drove one of those luxury vans, the kind you may remember from Marcia Brady's dates on *The Brady Bunch*. I didn't care though. I loved the fact that Todd was different from me, and that helped make it even more intriguing. I came to find out in the spring, he drove a different, sportier car, which—according to his parents—he never let anyone drive; but he let me. So I knew I had to be pretty special! We had so much fun together; but for sure, there were ups and downs in our relationship as well. This was an interesting time for me. I was really discovering a side of myself I didn't know. I learned that I liked the outdoors, and I liked the feeling of someone really liking who I was. Our relationship felt very genuine, and we dated all through the rest of college. We had countless conversations about love, and both of us seemed to be exploring its true meaning. As you may remember from what I said earlier, I was not allowed to date non-Jews, but I did tell my parents the truth this time and said Todd was not Jewish but that I really liked him. I didn't know how they would respond; but to my surprise, I don't remember there being any issue, for my parents met him and really liked him as well. I was thrilled to say the least because I felt, for the first time, my parents were seeing the person and not the religion. That was so important to me.

When we graduated, I moved to Virginia with a friend to try and find my first job, and Todd went back to Honeoye Falls to work in the family business. Although I majored in sociology and thought that I wanted to be a counselor of some sort, I wasn't quite ready for more school; and something was holding me back from pursuing the counseling field. Again, I think now, this was another sign from God and the hand He has had in all of this; but you will see this play out in what I believe to be my true purpose and calling in life.

I can remember the first time I drove from Ithaca to Honeoye Falls. Now this is a funny story. We didn't have cell phones or a GPS in our cars, so you had to actually use a map or written directions. I went with written directions, for map reading has never been my strength. Todd instructed me to follow the bend to the left after I passed Psycho Enterprise. I came to find out, it was actually called Cycle Enterprise. Then he told me to make a right at the light on East Street. Well I peered out of Ontario Street, saw the one light in town, and took the right and ended up in a town about a half hour from Honeoye Falls. I finally made it after flagging down a farmer on a tractor for directions. I guess it is hard to imagine getting lost in a town with only one traffic light. Now Todd could have thought or told me what a dummy I was, but I remember both he and his dad laughing about it and sort of thinking the whole thing was cute. This was like the beginning of someone seeing me differently than how my family saw me. No judgment was made about me as a person.

Again, this whole small-town thing was foreign to me. I would think to myself, *What do you do here for fun?* Fortunately, Todd and I dated long enough for me to find out. The Finger Lakes is an area that lends itself to boating in the summer and skiing in the winter. Fall is also another spectacular time in this area. All of these are things I got to experience as a result of dating the guy who was so different from me and not Jewish, the one who I met by chance that one day in a lecture called mental health issues. Starting to see God's hand in this?

In the summer of 1990, I decided to make the move to the Rochester area and join Todd. There was no more daily letter writing as that was what we did when we were apart. I have always had a love of writing but never thought that it would turn into me wanting to share my journey to God in a book. My parents seemed to be fine with my decision as I was supporting myself at this time with no help from them. Todd bought a duplex for us to live in, in East Rochester. I nannied and worked a random job in the city but felt the pull to do something that would be more secure. I knew I loved children; and so my first thought was I would become a teacher. I was fortunate enough to have the financial backing of my parents for grad school; and so I went on to grad school for education while Todd continued to work in the family business while getting his master's in finance. To help support myself, I worked as a hostess any chance I had. Between both of us in graduate school and working, we were very busy.

In the fall on October 12, 1991, Todd and I got engaged while on horseback in Vermont. It was such a memorable weekend, and we were so fortunate to be able to vacation in Vermont, for at the time, Todd's parents owned a home in Quechee. Todd's parents were very excited about our engagement and were waiting for us with champagne to celebrate it. I remember calling my parents to share the news, but they seemed most concerned with the size of the diamond I was given as opposed to how he asked me to marry him. Once again, the value of what was important was placed on the size of a diamond, not the fact that someone loved me and wanted to spend the rest of their life with me.

We would spend countless summers vacationing in the mountains of Vermont where we would golf, fish along the Connecticut River, and ride bikes. I believe this is where I began to really develop my love of being in the mountains. I always feel this sense of zen and an overwhelming sense of peace when I'm in the mountains. I believe in my heart, the mountains are where I feel most connected to God and His presence.

Because Todd had a much bigger extended family than me, and I was already living in the Rochester area, we decided to marry in Rochester and not Long Island. We chose the Interfaith Chapel at the University of Rochester for our ceremony where we would have his minister from the church he grew up at, and the only rabbi in the area who would perform Interfaith weddings at the time. He was a rabbi from Buffalo, and I remember meeting with him and discussing the notion of how we were going to raise the children. According to Jewish law, when you marry outside of your faith, the children take on the mom's religion, which would mean my children would be Jewish. I knew that this was very important to my parents, and I respected that; so after much discussion, Todd agreed that we would raise the children in the Jewish faith. Todd's parents were very accepting of this, and Todd loved me very much, and so he was willing to make this sacrifice for me. I, at the time, really had no idea of the sacrifice he truly was making because, in my eyes, it just meant our kids would grow up celebrating Hanukkah and some of the other Jewish holidays. Really, what would be the big deal? I had no idea what it meant to be a Christian because I thought Christianity just meant you celebrate other holidays that Jews didn't, like Christmas and Easter, and you believed in Jesus. I really did not know any meaning behind either of these, and I really didn't know the meaning behind following Christ.

Our wedding ceremony included both the Christian minister from Todd's Presbyterian Church and the rabbi from Buffalo. We did not get married under a traditional Jewish chuppah, but Todd did step on the glass (well a light bulb), signifying absolute finality in the covenant of marriage according to Jewish law. It also can represent the fragility of a relationship and the importance in preserving it. Once you hear the breaking of the glass, the guests yell, "*Mazel tov*" (congratulations), and at that point, we are able to kiss. We had a wonderful party celebrating with family and friends. My dad had the absolute time of his life. I remember him dancing the entire night and really having fun with all of our friends and really letting loose that night. It was probably the happiest I've ever seen him. There was an interesting moment at our wedding where my throw bouquet went missing, and so I got on the microphone—something I was happy to do—and I stalled for some time while they searched for the bouquet. It got to the point where I didn't know what else to say, and I remember our friend, Freddy, yelling to me, "Sing!" So I just started to sing a song that I sang growing up that my dad always liked called "You Light Up My Life" by Debby Boone, and all of a sudden, the band started to play along. It was another one of those amazing moments for me. Here I was at my own wedding, singing this song and not even realizing the meaning behind these lyrics and how God was really there at that moment telling me something. It was like He was reminding me of the true light that would someday lead my life as long as I would seek it. There is one verse in the song that says, "Alone in the dark, but now you've come along, and you light up my life, you give me hope to carry on." Again, I had no idea at the time the meaning behind these lyrics. But I have since learned that Debby Boone, the one who sang this song, also sang in a gospel quartet as her father was very religious. And when Debby was asked what she was singing about, she said God. Who would have ever imagined that at my wedding, I would be singing about the one thing I never even talked about my whole life. To me, this truly was another example of God's presence in my life. The trouble was, I had yet to know Him.

To be honest, when I think about Todd giving up the idea of raising his children as Christians, it makes me feel very bad knowing what I now know. However, I'm not sure that at the time, they would have grown up with more than Christian holidays at the center as Todd really never spoke of his relationship with God to me. Again, at the time, religion was based more to me on tradition, and I really didn't believe that either of us had any understanding of what it meant to be actively seeking faith and a relationship with the Lord. I figured, I can make the matzah ball soup and do all the traditional Jewish things I knew of. I would be a good Jew. But what I didn't realize was that my children would be missing out on something way bigger.

We started out having two children—first, Chandler in 1995, and then Emma in 1997. After having the two kids, we celebrated the Christian holidays as this was important to Todd and his family, and I wanted my kids to have that experience as well because Christmas and Easter celebrations were always about family. However, I made sure to have big Hanuhkah parties where Todd's parents, his grandma, and his aunt and uncle would attend. I would make the traditional potato latkes, which are potato pancakes, and I would try to make it a big deal because I knew once my kids got used to the idea of Santa, Hanukkah would seem like a boring holiday. Let me mention, at this point, we celebrated the holidays both Christian and Jewish, but God was not really a part of any of these celebrations. Todd's aunt would often pray at the dinner table at Christmas, and she would thank God for the food we were eating; but beyond that, we didn't really focus on the birth of Jesus and the importance of that. At this point, I really only associated God with dinner prayers and food. I also recited the Hebrew prayer each night when we lit the menorah on Hanukkah, and did so for the eight nights of Hanukkah. But again, these prayers were in Hebrew, and I have no idea what I was saying because praying in Hebrew was more of a rote thing I did. My kids were also learning to do these things because that was what good Jews should do. I never grasped the idea that God was a part of any of the prayers. As I am now writing this book, I've come to learn that the prayers were all about blessing God for His commandments, the miracles He has performed, and granting us life. These prayers, although beautiful, were certainly not going to teach me about how to talk to God. Yes, they were prayers about God, but talking about God in a rote way does not draw you closer to Him. Thanking God for the food we have on the table, I do not believe, draws you closer to Him either. What I began to see from both the Christian and Jewish holidays is that you do and say traditional things; but in reality, these things are not really how you get to know Him.

Chapter 3

CURIOSITY SPARKED

T odd and I had a lot of friends, and most of them celebrated the Christian holidays. I don't know what their relationship was like with God, but if asked, most of our friends would say they were Christians. Look carefully at that sentence regarding a relationship with God as this will be an important part of what I will be referencing along the way.

We had one family we were closest to. Over the years, we took vacations with them and did a lot of fun things together as families. My friend seemed to always have this certain peace about her. It may be that she was super laid back, but there seemed to be more to it. She was a very spiritual person. I remember that I would question her about the church she went to. She always talked about how fun the worship was, and she was very involved at the church, teaching Sunday school, and volunteering her time in many other realms. I was curious to say the least, for I had gone to the Presbyterian Church, but it felt very methodical to me; and the prayers seemed like they were the usual prayers that were recited each week. I never felt anything when I would attend a service, which I recall was usually a Christmas Eve service. Also, going to a service never appeared to be something Todd wanted to do either. It seemed like we were going out of duty on the few occasions when we did attend.

One day, I told my friend that I wanted to join her at a Sunday service. She was very excited that I had asked to do this. My friend never pressured me to do anything. When we would talk, she would listen to my concerns and just naturally share her thoughts and beliefs; but never once did she say, "You should do this" or "You should do that." The only thing she said was if I ever wanted to go to her church, she would be happy to bring me as a guest.

Up to this point, I did not have any spirituality, but there was something in me craving it. I would ask her a lot about her belief in God as she was always open to share it. The way she would radiate when speaking about God seemed so awesome to me. In my mind, I would always say, "I want that!" She would talk about Jesus as well, and that was always the part that was hardest for me. Growing up as Jewish, we did not talk about Jesus. I just knew that we were not supposed to believe that He was someone special as the Christians made Him out to be. Apparently, to Christians, He was the Messiah; and to Jews, we are still waiting for Him to come. The belief by Jews is that Jesus did not fulfill the messianic prophecies. Those prophecies are that he would build a third temple, gather Jews back to the land of Israel, create an era of world peace, and lastly, spread universal knowledge of the God of Israel uniting all under one God. Now I'm not sure if asked; most Jews would come up with these answers as to why they don't believe in Jesus. I think the most common thought is that most are told by their parents that they are not to believe in Jesus, and therefore, you didn't believe or worship Him growing up. This is a big part of religion in my mind. You are brought up with certain beliefs and very few people question them. My questions ultimately led me in the direction to find answers as to why I had no faith or spirituality and why I should not believe in Jesus. I remember that seeing images of Jesus on a cross or praying to Him made me uncomfortable. I never really understood why. It was like my mind was programmed to not accept Him as anyone other than someone who Christians worshiped. But I never took any time to really look into just who this Jesus was. I only knew that Jews didn't believe in Him, so I guess I wouldn't either.

I had passed Walnut Hill Community Church many times. This was the church my friend attended. It was a small, white barn, and it didn't scream church at all. It had a very quaint appearance because it was located on a country road, kind of in the middle of a farm. One Sunday, Todd the kids, and I joined my friend and her kids for a service. Of course, my kids were excited to see their friends, and Sunday school was fun for them as they were probably, at the time, five and three. I may be a little off on my dates and ages at this point, but the stuff that will really matter is quite accurate.

I remember pulling into the parking lot, and to my surprise, we saw many families we knew walking in. Everyone was so friendly and inviting. Chip Toth was the pastor at the time, and my friend made it a point to introduce us to him. He could not have been nicer, and we felt welcomed immediately. There was a worship band up at the front of the church, and the music was jamming as people were walking in and taking their seats. There also was a large screen; and once everyone was all settled, the lyrics to the songs would come up on the screen so that we could all sing along with the band. The musicians and the group of singers were amazing, and I remember it being so much fun. It was right up my alley as I loved to sing; and the music was really upbeat. I was not really paying much attention to the meaning of the lyrics, but I sure was singing away! I remember thinking to myself, *This is so different than any kind of worshiping I have ever been a part of.* It was as if everyone was so excited about God, and they were singing to Him with that excitement and thanks. After the worship time, we would all be seated, and Chip would now speak his message. Chip was a wonderful speaker and really used the word of God to lift you up and make you feel like, with God's power, anything was possible. As the service came to a close, I thought to myself, *I like this. It makes me feel good, and I want to learn more about it.* I felt like if I could just get over this Jesus thing, this might actually work for me. It was again God's hand in what was happening. I was being introduced to a place of worship, and I actually left feeling something. The music was motivating and uplifting, and we were singing to God in a way that I could understand. The sermon was funny, relatable, and used truths from the Bible and how they related to us as humans in everyday life. But then there was the Jesus thing. How was I going to pray to God in this church and ignore the Jesus thing? This was my challenge. And I wasn't sure just how I was going to get past it. God had a plan; and had I understood that at the time, I likely would have been more patient.

> The Lord is good to those whose hope is in him, to the one who seeks him; it is good to wait quietly for the salvation of the Lord. (Lamentations 3:25–26 NIV)

> Trust in the Lord with all your heart and lean not on your own understanding. (Proverbs 3:5 NIV)

> Now faith is confidence in what we hope for and assurance about what we do not see. (Hebrews 11:1 NIV)

> Therefore the Lord longs to be gracious to you. And therefore He waits on high to have compassion on you for the Lord is a God of justice; How blessed are all those who long for Him. (Isaiah 30:18)

We began attending Walnut Hill on a regular basis. I set up a meeting for Chip to come to our home so that I could discuss with him where I was on this journey in hopes that he would give me some insight into how to move forward. I feared the fact that I was really feeling something, like a pull to learn more; but this also meant that I was being drawn away from what I had always been taught to believe. I just didn't feel close to God in any way just because I made matzah ball soup on Passover. I had not had a positive temple experience, and I was still craving something in the spiritual realm. Again, my gut began directing me, and I knew I needed to gain a better understanding as to what was happening. Chip did a lot of listening. And when I reflect back to what we actually spoke about, I don't remember him ever saying do this or do that. It was almost as if he was instructing me to listen to God and take His direction. But I kept thinking, how do you do that when you don't know Him? My thought was maybe if I kept attending church, I would get to know Him because, clearly, those who were worshiping Him at church felt something. People would hold their hands up, close their eyes, and sing with such conviction, like they were saying, "Do you hear me God?"

I knew I was struggling with the Jesus part of this whole process; so one Saturday, I attended a service at a messianic temple in Rochester. At this temple, Jews believe in Jesus but keep their Jewish traditions and practices. There was a lot of dancing and singing, but I just did not feel connected in any way, and I remember feeling like that temple was not going to help me grow in my relationship with God. Again, my gut led me to this decision, and I continued to follow my gut in this whole process.

In June of 2002, we had our third child, Noah. I'll never forget his birth and the moment the doctor told me to reach down. I put my hands under his little arms and actually pulled him out and set him on my chest. It was the most amazing moment ever and one I will never forget! Noah was a true gift from God. At this point, we were attending church at Walnut Hill regularly; and it felt good. I loved going and felt like when I set out from a Sunday service, I was going to be able to conquer whatever came my way. Again, Chip always motivated us to feel that way because of the way he shared God's message. Other than attending church, I did not really delve into the Bible at this point. I was merely getting a taste of what it meant to worship God. We would sing to Him and listen to an inspiring message that came from passages in the Bible, but there was still this disconnect for me, a piece of the whole picture that I wasn't getting.

Eventually, I told Todd that I thought I might want to get involved with the church band and sing during the Christmas service. Todd was supportive and helped with the kids so that I could attend rehearsals and practices during the week. I remember feeling overwhelmed as I was not very good at harmonizing for it had been a long time since I actually sang, but I must have been good enough that they gave me a solo at Christmas time. It was a short solo but a solo nonetheless. For the life of me, I cannot recall the song; but I think it may have been "Go Tell It on the Mountain." We sang other songs like "Mary, Did You Know," "Away in a Manger," and so many other wonderful holiday songs. I can remember that night vividly from what I wore to the fact that my kids, my husband, and my in-laws were there watching me and even some friends who normally did not attend Walnut Hill. I worried so much about the evening as I was about to sing to God in front of a large worshiping audience. But little did I know, God was there guiding and directing me the whole way. Had I known that, I likely would not have worried the way I did.

> Do not be anxious about anything, but in every situation by prayer and petition, with thanksgiving, present your requests to God. And the peace of God, which transcends all understanding, will guard your hearts and your minds in Christ Jesus. (Philippians 4:6–7 NIV)

I knew in my heart, at this point, that I had a love for God, but I could not, for some reason, really love Jesus Christ the way I loved God. Who was this Jesus, and why did I need to believe in Him in order to grow closer to God? These were the questions I had and needed to find answers to. I figured that reading might help, and so I read a book called *Betrayed!* by Stan Telchin. It is about a girl who grows up Jewish and finds Christ and has to break the news to her parents. Her father begins to seek answers himself in hopes of proving her wrong, but what he learns truly changes the course of his life forever. I also started reading other books like *The Case for Faith* by Lee Stroebel and *Answering Jewish Objections to Jesus* by Michael Brown, and these books helped me to gain perspective, but I knew the real problem for me. I needed to share with my parents that I was questioning my faith, and that was a tough obstacle for me. I was stuck until I could share this. I guess you could say my faith in God wasn't quite there because had it been, I would have had the courage to face my parents.

For a moment in my life, I felt the need in my head to think about something that involved God. In my mind I remember thinking, *God, give me the strength and the confidence I need to send an email,* as that was how I decided I would tell them. So on July 12, 2003 at 3:15 a.m., I started to write the email to my parents. I began with, "Please know that anything I share with you is not meant to hurt you." I recapped a lot about my life growing up and how many times we as a family did things because it was what was expected as opposed to doing things from the heart. If we failed to send an anniversary card to my parents, we were made to feel badly about that. Or if we sent a gift that didn't meet their standards, they were sure to let us know they were unhappy. I shared how I felt the message about what was important in life was messed up in this way of thinking. Growing up, it was clear that my parents felt their way was the right way to do things; and other people were crazy if they lived differently. There was never any acknowledgment that everyone was entitled to live their life according to their own needs and beliefs. At this point in my life, I began to see outside of this box or way of thinking. It was almost as if it was okay to hurt other people's feelings because that was the way they did things. Because at this time, I had my own children, I would think to myself, *I would never want to hurt their feelings about anything, especially a gift they may have sent me.* I went on in the email about how much I appreciated all they have done for me as, monetarily, they definitely helped to make my life easy from paying for my college education and then paying for my graduate school as well. I believe those things were important to my parents. And if they accomplished them, in their minds, that made them good parents. But now that I was a parent, I was beginning to feel like there was more. And because I felt like spirituality and faith were missing in my life, I began to seek how to find that. So I continued to write, "I've learned that there is a difference between believing and being. I was being Jewish by cooking all the meals and celebrating as best I could with my family for the Jewish holidays. What was missing though was believing. What did I believe?" I mentioned the books I had read; about attending Walnut Hill; joining a Bible study, which began in the book of Genesis; and the fact that I believe that Jesus is the Messiah Jews have been waiting for. I ended the email asking them if they felt I should feel guilty for believing in God and wanting my children to grow up believing as opposed to being. I told them that I would want my children to learn about God but to ultimately choose on their own to be believers in Christ. I believe that making that choice as opposed to being told what to believe is what helps us all grow in our relationship with God.

So there it was. It was 5:00 a.m., and the send button was hit. I could remember feeling relief and a strange sense of strength. I did not anticipate that I would be receiving a loving email back, so the wait began. However, I had three kids and two who I had to get ready for school, so my mind was pretty preoccupied, and I didn't dwell on what was to come!

Well on July 13, the email came in all caps! I'm guessing the all-caps thing meant that my dad was angry. He questioned whether or not I followed Jewish traditions, if I kept my children out of school for Jewish holidays and taught my children about them, if I attended temple for Jewish holidays, if I associated with Jewish people, bought Jewish tapes for my children, read Jewish books like books about Anne Frank or the Holocaust, taught my children how to pray in the Jewish faith, and if I sent my kids to Jewish nursery school. He claimed that church or religion does not make a family closer, being good, respectful people is what counts. He told me to teach my children to be respectful and *not* get them involved in religion. Let's look at that statement: *not get my children involved in religion.* I was not aware that Judaism was not a religion. He also claimed that I didn't join a temple because I was too cheap and the Jewish religion cost money. He told me there was much more to life than religion. He went on to say that I was brainwashed by my leader. He said *I was following* the lovely journey of my leader, the *scripture*, and *Genesis* and that I *should forget about that and get a life.* He said I was not qualified to change religions. He said that I was giving up something I was born with given by God to find something else. He reiterated the fact that I should find Jewish friends and stay with Jewish people and give my kids an education on Jewishness. He told me that I was teaching my children what I thought was right but that it was one-sided. *He said I should open them up to other religions so they could make a choice.* He told me the title of my email should be "My poor, unhappy daughter who found a new life."

I knew I would need to reply to this email, and I waited a few days so that I could process what was shared by him. I reminded my father that I was not unhappy, depressed, or brainwashed. I simply had asked the question as to why Jews do not believe in Jesus, why God was not at the center of our beliefs, and in seeking my answers, I began to realize that many people of that ancient time did believe Jesus was the Messiah. Those who chose not to were bound by what they felt were laws that Jews were to abide by. I did not understand that people should merely accept being Jewish simply because that was how they were born. Just because you are born into a religion does not make that religion right. It was as if I was being instructed to associate with Jews so that I would never question being Jewish. I mentioned the point that my father said I should forget about scripture and Genesis, the first book of the Old Testament. So was my dad merely asking me to forget about the Bible and just be Jewish? According to the Torah, the issue is not one of a different religion but of lifestyle and faith. God is not concerned with what religion we identify with, but He is concerned with how we live and what we believe. The whole reason God sent Jesus was because people of that time were not living according to how God had anticipated people would. I learned that people were equating faith with their "works." People were sinning, and God sent Jesus so that people could confront their sins. Well there is much more to that idea from what I have learned while seeking my faith in God and not a religion.

So the email correspondences went back and forth for a few days. As I write about this now, I am certain I could not have gotten through all of this without the strength only one can get from God. In fact, I'm certain that this was the first time that God presented Himself to me, and I'm also certain it was because I was reaching out to *Him*. My father continued to berate me with the fact that I was being brainwashed. He continued to ask why I was unhappy.

He believed there were other ways of changing my life to bring about happiness but that believing in Jesus was not the answer. He reminded me of how lucky I was to have the husband I had, three healthy children, a beautiful home, a boat, a cottage, and that these things were given to me by God, not Jesus. I find this kind of interesting that in these emails, my father spoke so much about God, but growing up, not once can I remember the name of God ever being used in any way, shape, or form in English. We used the Hebrew word in prayer, Adonai, which meant God; but these were always rote prayers. We never actually spent time with God, for I would not have known what that looked like.

So from here, I moved forward with my decision; and I was baptized in Canandaigua Lake with my friend who brought me to Walnut Hill. It was a beautiful sunny day, and it was a really nice celebration; and I felt it was the beginning of a new journey for me. However, what I didn't know at the time was just how things would really play out in my life. This was the beginning of something but not really the true beginning of my relationship with God through Christ. At this point in my life, I was driven to develop my relationship; but all I took part in was weekly church services. I was not practicing my faith in other ways, and so I didn't really understand what I really needed to do, and shortly after this, our pastor left the church; and things got a little uncertain.

I got involved with a women's Bible study, and I tried to ask as many questions as I could. I think for many, they didn't understand the place I was coming from. In their minds, we were studying Genesis, the first book of the Bible in the Old Testament, and I should be familiar with it. However, I really wasn't. I mean, I knew the story of Adam and Eve, but I really didn't have a good understanding beyond that. God had big plans for me, and I just needed to remain patient. As we all learn, as practicing Christians, God does things on His time, not on ours!

> The Lord is good to everyone who trusts in
> him, so it is best for us to wait in patience—to
> wait for him to save us - And it is best to learn

this patience in our youth. (Lamentations 3:25–27 NIV)

Lean on, trust in, and be confident in the Lord with all your heart and mind and do not rely on your own insight or understanding. In all your ways know, recognize, and acknowledge Him, and He will direct and make straight and plain your paths. (Proverbs 3:5–6)

∞

Chapter 4

WHERE DO I
FIND GOD?

Our time at Walnut Hill was cut short after Chip, the pastor, left. We stayed on and tried to support the church with the acting pastor, but things seemed to be falling apart at the seams, and people began leaving and looking for other places to worship. Our next stop was Crosswinds Wesleyan Church in Canandaigua, New York. After attending a church in what was practically a barn, this seemed like a whole different experience. Crosswinds had a huge band, big screens, lights, and a huge auditorium in which to worship. The church was very well-run from children's programs to welcoming committees to all sorts of ministries. It was a lot to take in after coming from a small, little church that felt more like a home.

After some time, our kids began complaining about attending church, and that made the half-hour commute to Canandaigua one which was becoming a total drag. Todd and I loved the sermons and the worship time, so we fought the battle with our children and continued to attend. The pastor really seemed to connect with the congregation and spoke about topics that were very relatable from the Bible. However, my connection with God just was not where I thought it should be. It was as if I was going through all the motions of singing, taking in the sermons, and attending church every Sunday, but it was as though Monday through Saturday, God was not present. I began to rely on the pastor to really grow my faith; but truly, that was not going to be the way I would grow and mature as a Christian. However, at this time, I didn't realize it at all. I had thought that going to church is what makes you a Christian; and if you define yourself as one, then you will automatically have that relationship with God.

We attended Crosswinds for a few years, but then our children got involved in youth football and cheerleading. These events were held on Sunday; and so instead of worshiping, we spent Sundays cheering for our football player and our cheerleader. Our church life became one in which we would attend on Christmas Eve and Easter. My search for God seemed to come to a halt, although I still identified with being a Christian as I believed in Jesus but didn't truly have a good understanding in how to worship God through Him. So the question kept creeping up: Why if I believe in Jesus do I not really feel like God is present in my life? I had this longing and question in my mind but didn't really know who to ask or how to go about finding out the answer to this question. Many of the friends I had attended church as well, and some served in ministries. That led me to the idea that maybe if I got involved in a ministry, that would be the answer. So I got involved in the welcome ministry for a bit and served as a greeter, but God didn't seem to meet me there either. There were times where I just felt maybe God didn't want to know me because no matter how much I would attend church, He never really seemed to be there to greet me. So if church isn't the path to finding God, celebrating the holidays in honor of Christ isn't the way to connect with God, singing and worshiping aren't connecting me to God, then what will?

Life just moved along. Holidays came and went, and my kids kept me pretty busy. However, there were moments in my life where I wasn't sure what I was supposed to be doing. I mean, I loved being a mom, but I was missing something.

A friend of mine was teaching at a local private Jewish school, and she told me that a teacher was ill, and they were in need of a long-term sub. The position was covering for a teacher who taught sixth, seventh, and eighth grade social studies. Now I had experience teaching social studies but only at the sixth-grade level. But because this was a private school, I could teach outside of my certification. A little side note here, when I told my parents about me teaching social studies, their comment to me was, "You are going to teach social studies. How are you going to teach social studies when you didn't do well at it in high school or even like it?" Again, the lack of encouragement was astonishing at times. I went on to have the interview with the rabbi (principal) and another woman, and I was offered the position. This really was interesting to me because here I was, a woman born a Jew, converted to Christianity, and now here I am, back teaching at a Jewish school. One may say, another part of God's plan and presence in my life. The children were pretty challenging. They did not accept my style of teaching at first as their other teacher was more of a "read these pages and answer these questions" kind of teacher. That was not me at all! I loved getting them to be creative and use creative ways to demonstrate their knowledge. For example, I asked them to develop a political campaign for a person we studied and obviously based on what they learned, they would be able to do that. This required a bit more collaboration in a group setting and also required them to think a bit outside of the box. I can clearly remember an incident in the first week I was there. I walked into my classroom, and on my desk was a note taped to my desk saying, "You are Satan." Interestingly enough, the note was written by one of the administrator's children. I can really remember dreading each day at this school. First off, I had to drop my little two-year-old Noah off at an in-home day care. This was not easy for me especially since I can recall how when I would drop off and pick up, many of the older children would be sitting in front of the TV. Because of the sadness and anxiety I had about first, leaving Noah and second, going to this school where the kids were so mean, I began doing something I never had done before. I began talking out loud in my car to God. I would drive in my car, and I would ask God to give me the ability to get through another day. I would ask that He give me the confidence to not allow these children to try and control my classroom and to remain confident in how I was asking them to learn regardless of them fighting me every step of the way. As the weeks passed, the kids in all three grade levels seemed to begin to enjoy the group activities, and I actually was beginning to feel like they were starting to like me. Every morning in the car, I would drop Noah off and start my conversation with God. I had no idea at the time that this was actually called praying. If you recall, the only praying I was accustomed to was praying over food. I do vividly remember feeling like my talks with God were helping me to get through this job. What I had yet to learn is the importance of not talking and just listening to God.

Let's get back to the notion that this was a Jewish school, and therefore I had a lot of questions that I felt could be answered by the teachers there who were teaching Jewish history and other Jewish courses. There was one day when I was in my room, planning, and a teacher came in to do some work. I remember thinking to myself, *I'm going to use this time to dig a little deeper for my own personal reasons.* I asked the teacher if he minded me asking him some questions about his beliefs. In his Jewish accent, he replied sure. So I just came out with the question as to why he and other Jews do not believe in Jesus. I don't remember exactly how he answered the question, but I remember him saying that Jesus did not fulfill the Messianic prophecies. Unfortunately, at this time, I was not as well versed in the Bible and could not therefore dig deeper. However, I left the conversation not really feeling convinced that what he shared was true. I felt like our conversation really was reflective of what I had come to learn about my Jewish upbringing. You are told not to believe in Jesus and to live your life sticking to Jewish law. In addition, you are expected never to question this.

I finished out my long-term subbing there and celebrated the fact that I did something truly outside of my comfort zone by teaching history at a level that I was not trained to teach in. I also recognized for the first time the notion of placing my trust in God. I sort of felt His presence on every car ride, and it truly strengthened me as I tackled each day. It was the first time I think I consciously thought about God in a way that, if I asked something of Him, I might be blessed by Him. However, my conversations were with God, not

Jesus. I didn't really understand Jesus's role at this point, but I knew I had to believe in Him in order to make my way to God. And for the first time, I recognized that God was in my life even though I was not at church. This was something very new for me because when I began my journey, I didn't really understand that God was always with me, and I could talk or pray to Him at any time.

Shortly after this position ended, I received a phone call from the director of a local preschool. My daughter, Emma, had attended this school, and the director had remembered a conversation we had had about my having been a teacher. She was calling to see if I would consider being a lead teacher in their pre-K class. My initial thought was, *How am I going to teach preschoolers?* I had really only been a sixth-grade teacher up to this point other than the subbing job I had recently had at the Jewish school. I was also concerned about my Noah. He was going to be attending the school two days a week for their three-year-old program, and then what would I do the other two days? I'd love to be able to say I prayed about it, but I was not that mature yet as a Christian, so I did what most humans do. I talked to my husband; I talked to my friends; and I decided that if I found someone for Noah who could come to my home for two mornings, then I would do it. Well wouldn't you know that God had His hand in this one too. A sitter basically fell into my lap and next thing I knew, I was leading a pre-K class.

I had a wonderful assistant at the time who had been in the classroom prior to me arriving, and she was extremely fun to work with and so very supportive. We made a great team, and I really enjoyed teaching that age group. I loved the parent involvement and everyone at the school, especially my director who was just wonderful. My director and I developed a very special relationship. She was a very faithful God-loving woman, and she was not only a mentor to me at the school, but I felt as though she was a mentor to me in life as well. She was one of the first people I had ever met who openly talked about the role God played in her life and shared a lot about her faith with me. There was just an angel-like aura that she possessed. You could feel very stressed about something, but then she would walk into my room, and there was this wonderful peace in her presence.

I loved my job, and I loved working at the school; but the next year, things did not work out for me to work there. We were in the middle of building a new home, and I did not have anyone to watch Noah. I left on great terms as my director always was of the mindset that family comes first. The next couple of years, I went back into my role as mom. I volunteered in my kids' classrooms, and I took care of "mom things." We didn't really stay involved in any church at this time. Another pastor had come and gone at another church, and our kids squawked at the mention of going. And then of course, in the summer we were at the lake, and church did not appear to fit into our life. It felt as though life was getting busy, and my walk with God appeared not to be front and center. I believe now that until you realize the role God plays in your life, you are less likely willing to commit to building a relationship with Him.

A few years went by, and we really were not invested in our faith as a family at all. We weren't even attending church for holiday services at this point. Every so often, I would catch Joyce Myers on a TV show, and I would feel uplifted by her message. But my heart was not where it needed to be to seek God. In fact, I was lost in who I was. Being a full-time, at-home mom can do that to you. I had an overwhelming sense of being something, but that something did not seem valued by anyone, including me. I was needed by everyone in my family, but the tasks I did on a daily basis were not growing me as a person. Had I known then what I know now about God, my life from this point on would not have been turned upside down the way it did for a period of time. I would have sought God's wisdom, and I would have had confidence that God was there listening to me. Instead, I chose to find validation by others in the wrong way and came very close to ruining my marriage and hurting the one person in my life who has loved me more than anyone ever has. I guess the saying holds true that you really can't love completely until you love yourself, and I didn't love myself so I couldn't imagine anyone loving me either. The other part of this is that sometimes we go through trials, and that's where we are met by God.

Love is such an interesting concept and one that has taken me a long time to really and truly understand. When you grow up with the notion of what love is the way I did, I think you get all confused by what the term love really means.

How love was presented to me growing up was through the buying and giving of things. These are the kinds of gestures that were meant to make you feel loved and therefore assume you were loved. The words were never spoken, and the warmth of a hug was never felt, but I was given things; and because of that, I was supposed to know I was loved. Truly, love is such a complex term with such a big feeling associated with it. I craved to be loved in so many ways. I sought it through friendships and relationships. But what I did not realize is that God loved me; and with His love, all things are possible.

> Jesus looked at them and said, "With man this is impossible, but with God all things are possible." (Matthew 19:26)

It's interesting because the kind of love from God is displayed so differently. Living in the flesh makes this thing called love so confusing. Everyone seems to love and show love differently. My husband's aunt displayed love through these amazing hugs that you would never forget because they were like no other. My mother-in-law is such an amazing listener, and so you can feel her love through that and by always being there to listen and show she cares. For me, I found the ability to share my love through the written word, which is ironic that I have taken to the written word to share my story and my love of God. I may not be the most profound writer out there, but whenever I have something heavy on my heart, I seem to want to write.

Back to my experience with love, I think, based on life experiences with how we are loved, we begin to go through our lives not questioning it, and we usually just repeat what was learned. However, for me, this didn't seem right. What I began to recognize was that giving could be a form of showing love unless something was expected in return. With that concept in mind, when I was given something, I was expected to do something in return. It was sort of like the notion that I did this for you, so what are you going to do for me?

I think this played out in my life for some time. I was very caught up in doing things not in a humble way but for the recognition. My thought notion of love was, "I do this for you, and you then do this for me." One example that stands out in my mind was the day of my wedding. As tradition would have it, a bride is supposed to wear something old, something new, and something blue. My something new was a set of pearls with pearl earrings that were given to me by my mother. I remember receiving these pieces of jewelry, and I really don't remember feeling like they were given out of love. I remember feeling like I was supposed to make a big deal about them because my mother *did this for me*. I also remember being very caught up in "my" day; and apparently, my reaction to them was not what it should have been in my mother's eyes. And instead of it being a moment of love, it became more of a "look what I did for you moment."

As I reflect on this idea, what I began to notice is how selfish love can make us and how caught up in the flesh we can get. Again, these sorts of moments really have revealed themselves to me because I believe God's hand has been in this process the whole time. Sometimes it truly takes the trials in our lives to help us to see the bigger picture.

Chapter 5

LIFE WITHOUT THE PRESENCE OF GOD

It's always interesting to fast-forward my life and reflect on how ugly my life was without seeking God. I tried to fool myself into believing that I was trying to find ways to look for God, but I was not committed to the search for Him. I was trying to keep my head afloat with all the kids' activities and running the house; so when Todd got home from work, there was a sense of calm. I have to be honest, with three kids and a husband trying to run a company, it is oftentimes hard to find calm in that kind of chaos. Even though I was busy running the kids to where they needed to go, I began to lose a little sense of myself, and God was not at the forefront of my life. I became that person who didn't take the time to seek God, and my life took a turn for the worse. I became a person who really just lost a sense of who I was and began to feel as if I was not good at anything. It became like an overwhelming sense of worthlessness.

We began struggling with a child who was having anger issues, and my husband and I were on different pages. He had his opinion as to how we should handle the issues, and I had mine. Our home was not calm, but we managed to find ways to have those great family moments. Many of those moments were shared at our cottage on

Keuka Lake. It is amazing how you can feel so much better when you are surrounded by things that only God created. I guess you could say that maybe that was my reminder to look closely, and I would see that God was always there.

With all three kids involved in sports, it became hard during the school year to eat family dinners and just have that downtime. Life became a whole lot of rushing here and there and dividing and conquering as to who would be at what game. For me, I also began to allow feelings of envy and failure to creep in. I would compare myself to other moms who seemed to have it altogether. Their houses were always clean, proper wreaths for the season were on the door, flowerpots filled, their kids seemed to have it altogether, and their kids were the best athletes. I harbored those feelings and felt as though maybe I was not doing a good job at being a mom. However, what I failed to realize was that everyone was really pretty much in the same boat, and I just assumed these things because on the outside, people could make their lives look pretty perfect. However, no one really knows what goes on behind closed doors. Today this kind of thing is at the forefront of people's lives as we stay glued to our phones, on Instagram, and Facebook. Again, I realize the importance today of sharing the truths of the Bible so that my children can recognize the true meaning of love and how to best live their lives not according to their phones but according to how Jesus lived his.

During this time, I was slowly becoming a person that was allowing Satan to creep into every part of me that was vulnerable because I was in a place without God. My life felt as though it was spiraling out of control. Had I recognized that God was there or if I had had friends who were mature Christians who I could have sought out for Christian advice, my choices may have been different. Instead, I handled things the way many do without seeking the counsel of God. His message and words were there for me, but I didn't know how to seek them or use them. I didn't have a Bible, yet even if I did, I would not have known what to do with it. No one around me was speaking the word of God, and I was really at rock bottom in how I was feeling about myself.

During this time in my life, I was so far removed from God that I began to become a person that even I would not have recognized. I am now able to see that this was Satan's way of moving me farther away from God, which is where he wanted me. I became a selfish and unloving person and hurt the *one* person in my life who has *truly* loved *me*, my husband. What became clear to me is that forgiveness is something we all struggle with, and the struggle for me was learning to forgive myself. God was going to teach me what it means to forgive, and the lesson was going to include the notion that when we believe in Jesus, we can rest assure that our sins were forgiven on the cross.

> For if you forgive other people when they sin against you, your heavenly Father will also forgive you. (Matthew 6:14 NIV)

> Blessed is the one whose transgressions are forgiven, whose sins are covered. (Psalm 32:1 NIV)

> If we confess our sins, he is faithful and just to forgive us our sins and to cleanse us from all unrighteousness. (1 John 1:9 NIV)

> Love prospers when a fault is forgiven, but dwelling on it separates close friends. (Proverbs 17:9 NIV)

> The Lord our God is merciful and forgiving, even though we have rebelled again Him. (Daniel 9:9 NIV)

> He has delivered us from the power of darkness and conveyed us into the Kingdom of the Son of His love, in whom we have redemp-

tion through His blood, the forgiveness of sins.
(Colossians 1:13–14 NIV)

Fortunately, I had a committed husband who loved me and fought for our marriage. I began to learn a lot about myself during this time and a lot about what it meant to truly be loved. Not really having grown up in a loving environment and having had a lot of criticism along the way really affected my confidence in who I was. I therefore became insecure about the kind of mother, wife, and even friend I was.

Then one day, the phone rang again. We still had a home phone at this time, and I can remember lifting the portable phone to my ear and hearing the sound of my director's voice from the preschool. She was calling again to see if I would have any interest in teaching the pre-K class again at the preschool. With three kids all in school, before she could ask the next question, my answer was yes! God sure knew just what I needed, and I believe truly that again this was just another part of his plan.

Going back to teaching was the best thing for me. It allowed me to look outside of myself and use the gifts God gave me to do something rewarding. I ran with it! I spent countless hours trying to plan the very best lessons, and I always loved presenting things in class. To me, teaching was almost like a form of acting. The classroom was the stage; and because I was teaching four- to five-year-olds, I could do silly things, make up silly songs, and just have fun! Some of my most memorable moments were doing rap songs with preschool lyrics. My son, Noah, had one of those electric portable beat things and so I would create a beat, and we would sing away.

Now I was definitely feeling more self-worth and loving my day-to-day, but I was not spending a lot of time thinking about the role God was playing in my life. I definitely can see now how when things are going well in your life, you forget about God; and when things are not going so well, you tend to want Him to be there. However, until you make a practice of this, you really don't recognize the role God is playing in your life. Even now, as I write this book, I see the intertwining of God's presence in my life. But because I was not fully committed, I never really grasped the meaning of what it means to follow Christ.

My pre-K class became very popular in the community I lived in. We always capped out at twelve students, and I was so blessed with another great assistant. She and I had the best time teaching together. She was the soft-spoken kind voice in the classroom, and I was the loud, crazy teacher who cared for those kids more than anything. I began teaching the pre-K class for the second time in 2010 and really began perfecting the program. Things were really going well until the following school year in 2012 when we were faced with some terrible news. The director of our school was ill with cancer. She had the most positive attitude about it as it was not her first run with cancer, but things were tough. In October of 2013 she passed away. And besides being devastated that we had lost this angel-like person, we also had to come to grips with who would run the school.

I had considered this a possibility. And at her service, I told her husband that I would consider taking over for her, and he seemed happy with the news. However, that thing called lack of confidence crept in again, and I feared doing this on my own. Another teacher at the school and I began talking about the possibility of running it together. It seemed like the perfect solution. It began on a high note as we shared the responsibility of the director's role. But as the year progressed, things seemed to be falling apart. We had never really identified the responsibilities she would have or ones I would have, and that started to become an issue.

However, we moved forward for the next year, and I was going to have a new classroom so that I could have more space with new tables and take on two more students. I was so excited about that part as was my assistant. I spent time over the summer setting up my classroom using a polka dot theme, and it looked amazing. Name tags lined the halls, the alphabet filled the walls, and it just felt so perfect; and I was so excited about the year. However, summer was a busy time for the paperwork, and things became apparent that the codirector and I were not going to be able to make things work. Again, I could have prayed about it, but instead, I used people to guide and direct me. I guess I was of the world at this point and not in the world.

> Do not love the world or anything in the world. If anyone loves the world, love for the Father is not in them. For everything in the world—the lust of the flesh, the lust of the eyes, and the pride of life—comes not from the Father but from the world. The world and its desires pass away, but whoever does the will of God lives forever. (1 John 2:15–17 NIV)

I called for a board meeting, but our board was made up of all employees of the school, which really caused people to not want to say too much in fear that they could lose their job or create hostility for them. I finally turned to a friend who understood what a board was and told him what was happening. His recommendation after all I shared was to resign and make it effective immediately. So I went home, drew up a letter, shared with my husband what I was about to do and made my resignation effective immediately just as I had been advised.

I was heartbroken! The program I had worked years to create would not be taught by me. I had to share with all the families that I was not going to be their children's teacher. I truly cried for days and was completely in disbelief that this was what it came to. I can remember meeting a former teacher who was there to watch me as I took down all of the things I had created for my wonderful classroom. They had to have someone there to make sure I only took what was mine. I felt like I had done something terribly wrong when, in fact, I really felt for the first time in my life that what I had done for that school was something wonderful. We had a program that was highly recognized in the community, and it was a program that I created and really personalized. It was just a horrible day, and I packed up my whole classroom and placed it all in big plastic tubs. To this day, they all sit in my barn because I literally can't part with all of the lessons, the laminated pictures, and letters I made. Even now, I can get teary-eyed thinking or even writing about it. I was Heidi the preschool teacher, and now who was I going to be?

The sad part about this is knowing what I know now, which is that I could have had more strength if I had had more faith. I could have gotten through this so much easier if I had trusted that things really do happen for a reason, and it would be revealed to me on God's time. However, I didn't really have any of that. Maybe it was sort of there, but I didn't have the tools necessary to figure out how to use God at this moment. At this point, I was lost.

Chapter 6

GOD KNOWS JUST WHEN TO STEP IN

September 2014 came, my kids went back to school, the preschool found another teacher, and I moved on as best I could.

One morning, I was sitting at the kitchen counter, scrolling through Facebook, and I saw a post about a ladies' group starting. I read on, and a woman in my community talked about how she and two other women were going to lead a ladies' group. The idea would be to read a book that was biblically sound, and then as a group, we would have a discussion on the book, and we would meet weekly. I had known the leader of the group, Kelly, for many years as our boys played flag football together. She was a woman who I was always intrigued by. I remember thinking, *Wow, that woman has four beautiful kids, and she is so pretty.* Her children had attended a local Christian school; and so I only saw her for football and basketball games. We would always chat, which I loved to do because she had the cutest Southern Alabama accent, but we never did more than chat on the sidelines. At any rate, I knew that the group would be faith based because Kelly always quoted scripture on her Facebook posts, and I just felt very excited to join this group because I was in a very bad place with the loss of my preschool career; and I felt a big pull to do this. This certainly was outside of my comfort zone on many levels. One, I was not always comfortable meeting with a group of strangers, and two, I didn't really know anything about the Bible. However, I really felt convicted to give it a try. Little did I know that this would be a life-changing decision for me, and I believe God knew this the whole time.

The group would meet Tuesday mornings from 9:00 to 11:00 a.m. The book we were going to read was called *Breaking Free* by Beth Moore, and Kelly had quoted something regarding verses that kept reappearing about Jesus calming the storm. I knew I was in the middle of a storm, so what she was writing about resonated with me. She went on to write, "Christ does not always immediately calm the storm, but He is always willing to calm His child based on His presence. 'Don't worry! I know the winds are raging and the waves are high, but I am God over both. If I let them continue to swell, it's because I want you to see Me walk on the water.'" She went on to say that "we may never learn to enjoy our storms, but we can learn how to enjoy God's presence in the storm"(*Breaking Free*, Beth Moore). Well if this wasn't something I needed to hear, then I don't know what greater role God was playing here.

I messaged Kelly back letting her know that I was interested in joining the group, and I had planned on ordering my book. I shared with Todd that I had planned to do this, and he was supportive of my decision to do so. Interestingly enough for me, in my life, I have always felt guilty about taking time for myself as I have always had guilt about not working and contributing financially; but for whatever reason, I had no guilt about this. This I knew was going to be for me. But God for sure had way bigger plans here, and what I'm about to share is the best way God works in our lives as long as we welcome Him.

It was early September 2014, Tuesday morning, almost 9:00 a.m., and I set off to Kelly's house with my book *Breaking Free* in hand. I had a sort of nervous excitement about going to this ladies' group. Kelly greeted me at the door, and women came in gradually. One of the women was someone I knew, so that helped bring comfort to an uncomfortable situation for me. We chatted a bit in the kitchen with some small talk and slowly made our way to the family room where we sat with books in hand around the perimeter of Kelly's family room. I admit though, I was happy to see a familiar face, but I was also concerned about sharing things in front of people who sort of knew me in the community.

The meeting began with introductions of who we were, a little about ourselves, and what drew us to the ladies' group. My turn came, and I remember sharing with tears in my eyes the difficulty I had been facing with my resignation from the preschool. I went on to share how I was ready to be called by God to break free from the thoughts and feelings I was experiencing from this event in my life. I was excited to begin my journey to seek out the obstacles that were preventing me from living a life of freedom in God. I was ready to break free of the strongholds that had grasped so tightly around me that I couldn't see past them. I was ready to get to know God and believe Him, glorify Him, find satisfaction in Him, experience His peace, and enjoy His presence (Beth Moore, *Breaking Free*). To do this I was also ready to access my unbelief, my pride, my idolatry, my prayerlessness, and my legalism (Beth Moore). I was ready to confront the things that Beth Moore described as obstacles that block our access to what God can do in our lives. I was beginning to see that this study was about to reveal to me how to really tap into God through the salvation of Jesus Christ. Beth Moore explained it with great simplicity. She described how I had to recognize I was a sinner. We all carry a sense of great pride in ourselves. And to recognize you are a sinner, you need to really let go of that pride. This, for sure, was step one. Second, I had to acknowledge that Jesus Christ is the Son of God, and I can only be saved through Him. I still was not sure what that meant at the time, but I was ready to learn. Third, I had to believe that Jesus died for my sins, and His death was on my behalf. That truly was a big one. There was no one I could ever imagine in the human realm that would be so willing to sacrifice themselves so unconditionally. This truly spoke to just who Jesus Christ had to be. And lastly, I needed to be able to say, "My life is Yours, Jesus, so please be my Lord and my Savior." I believed in my heart this was truly what I needed next in my walk with God. I had been taking so many little steps toward trying to have faith, and I believed in my heart that this next chapter was going to be the most revealing of all, both on a personal level and a spiritual one too.

At this point, I recognized the work that I would need to do to really live my life glorifying God. I would need to reveal God through my life and the way I live, and that was something I hadn't really grasped. That's not to say that I wouldn't mess up because I am, again, only human, and that is why God came to earth in human form to begin with. What a mess our humanness was. People thought laws would guide and make their paths right, but they failed to take into account the notion of pride and other human qualities that caused us to get off course. Jews of ancient times viewed sacrifice as a way of making themselves right with God, but what God really wanted was for humans to live their day-to-day honoring Him in how we act toward others and how we truly live our lives. Again, this takes me back to my recollection of what it means to be a good Jew who makes their matzah ball soup on Passover. Forming those balls of matzah meal never once made me think about God, and it certainly did not glorify God in any way. God was never concerned about traditions especially if the traditions fail to really honor Him. I made the matzah balls so I could tell my parents, "Yes," when they asked, "Heidi, did you make your matzah ball soup?" This usually furthered the discussion as to whether or not they were hard or soft. Don't get me wrong, the story behind the meaning of Passover is truly a beautiful part of history, but what I was beginning to come to terms with was that history tells a story; and as children of God, we have a greater responsibility other than to take part in celebrations that honor that history. Learning about history through the truths in the Bible was how I was going to honor God. I was about to learn that I needed to submit myself to God and truly believe and trust that He was in control of my life. My true surrender to God would lead me from emotion to obedience. It was through this obedience that I would be led from the struggles we face as humans in our world filled with so much strife. Although this sounds easy, it requires so much discipline and trust that it at times seems unnatural.

As I mentioned, sitting amongst a group of women I mostly didn't know was not my strong suit. Don't get me wrong, I'm pretty outgoing and can talk to others easily; but because I still struggle with myself, so to speak, there was always the small worries: Would I say something "dumb"? Would I share too much about myself? Would I be knowledgeable enough to even share anything? These are just some of the thoughts that I could have allowed to have held me captive. But God clearly had another plan for me; and so week after week, I would attend our Tuesday morning time from nine to eleven.

We always opened up in prayer, and Kelly was a wonderful facilitator. She always had a cute little personal story to relate to the direction our discussion was headed in, or she merely would have us do a little icebreaker from time to time. I think, honestly for me, I was so inspired by Kelly's commitment to her love of the Lord that I just wanted to have what she had. I think that curiosity really drove me to come week after week. As I write about the word *Lord*, I thought to myself, prior to this journey, I never thought about the use of the term *my Lord*. These were the kinds of changes that came as a result of seeking. I remember how those in the group would interchange the terms *Father* and *Lord*. I understood the idea of God the Father and praying to God was something I could do, but the Lord thing was new to me. If you recall from an earlier chapter or time in my journey, I spoke of the obstacle I had with understanding Jesus and how I would learn to know Him and what His role would be in growing my faith. Up until this time, Jesus to me was the man who died on the cross. But I really didn't understand who He was and the whole significance of Him dying on the cross and what being resurrected meant. Even though our study was about breaking free from the things in life that held us captive, I was about to learn that what was really keeping me captive was not understanding Jesus and how, through Him, I would be set free. Jesus is my Lord and my Savior, and it is through Him that I have grown closer to God.

Looking back, it is clear to me that as a Jew, I was taught tradition and events in history that only related to Jews. However, one big event that seemed to never be addressed was the birth of a baby named Jesus. Jesus was born a Jew, and they called him rabbi in the

Bible, but I wondered why I was taught to hold such angst toward this Jew. Why was it such a blatant attack on Judaism to question who Jesus was, yet to others He is such an integral part of their life? These were the kinds of questions I was ready to learn the answers to.

At the start of my married life, I accepted a teaching position as a sixth-grade teacher, and one of the core subjects I taught was social studies. It was ironic because I never really liked history at all growing up. I can remember little about American history class other than my teacher always wore a blouse every Friday that had the world map on it, and the girl I sat next to in class always fell asleep. However, I got hired to teach social studies; and at the sixth-grade level, the curriculum focuses on global history beginning with the ancient civilizations. I bring this up only to tie in the idea that history is of such great importance that we teach it in school. However, for whatever reason, this part of history in relation to religion was never really explained, nor was I ever encouraged to learn about it or raise any questions about it. When students would ask me why we learn about history, I would tell them that we learn about the past and the way people did things long ago so that we can grow from it and not make the same mistakes of those who had already been through something in the past. In addition, we can take from our history and live better lives using the knowledge of our ancestors and their achievements. However, the question still lurks as to why, as a Jew, I was never encouraged to do that with this part of history. Ironic here was that what I taught my sixth graders to do was exactly what I began to do on my own. I was trying to understand history so that I could grow and use the knowledge learned to better my own life.

So week after week in my ladies' group, we would read our book *Breaking Free*, and Beth Moore would discuss the great importance of God's presence in our life. What I was about to discover was the way I would finally have that relationship with God.

Chapter 7

HI, I'M JESUS, GLAD TO MEET YOU, HEIDI

In order to understand who Jesus really was, I think it is pertinent to go back to the book of Isaiah in the Old Testament.

> Therefore the Lord himself will give you a sign: The virgin will conceive and give birth to a son, and will call him Immanuel. (Isaiah 7:14)

> For to us a child is born, to us a son is given, and the government will be on his shoulders. And he will be called Wonderful Counselor, Mighty God, Everlasting Father, Prince of Peace. (Isaiah 9:6)

> No one living in Zion will say, "I am ill", and the sins of those who dwell there will be forgiven. (Isaiah 33:24)

> Forget the former things; do not dwell in the past. (Isaiah 43:18)

He grew up before him like a tender shoot, and like a root out of dry ground. He had no beauty or majesty to attract us to him, nothing in his appearance that we should desire him. He was despised and rejected by mankind, a man of suffering, and familiar with pain. Like one from whom the people hide their faces he was despised, and we held him in low esteem. Surely he took up our pain and bore our suffering, yet we considered him punished by God, stricken by him, and afflicted. But he was pierced for our transgressions, he was crushed for our iniquities; the punishment that brought us peace was on him, and by his wounds we are healed. (Isaiah 53:2–5)

At this point, anyone reading this must be saying to themselves, "If this was prophesied in the Old Testament—and clearly who they are talking about is Jesus—then why do Jews not believe Jesus was the Messiah? At this point in my writing, I needed to step back and google a lot so that I would have some understanding as to what was going on. Why wasn't I told this? Why did I never know of this?

What I had learned was, in the seventeenth century, rabbi's took it upon themselves to remove Isaiah 53 altogether. When this book in the Old Testament is being referenced to Jews, they literally skip over the fifty-third chapter. So what I have concluded is this: I never learned about Jesus not because He was someone bad or good. He was taken out of Jewish belief because there were people living during this time that simply did not want to believe who He was, and that is what has been passed down for thousands of years. Jews believe the servant, spoken of by Isaiah, to be the people of Israel. But if you look into this, it cannot be true.

Rabbi Rettig claims that the prophecy of Isaiah 53 is not about the Messiah but about Israel, that gave itself up as an innocent lamb, can we really say that the people of Israel could be

described as "an innocent lamb"? Innocent lamb
is a Biblical definition for one without sin, who
is blameless, spotless, never does evil and would
never sin, but is perfect, pure and clean from sin.
Do the people of Israel really fit this description?
(oneforisrael.org)

As a result, there are people all across this world missing out on
truth and spirituality because laws trumped belief. The trouble with
this really being true is the fact that even in historic times, Jews followed the laws of sacrifice. But God knows everyone's heart. He saw
that Jews were sacrificing lame animals, and that really means that
these sacrifices were not from the heart.

It's interesting because when I think back to how I was parented, I was never really encouraged to question anything. It could
be a rule my parents had, an opinion they may have held—really just
about anything. Another aspect of what I have observed over time
is you can share your opinion, but it is their opinion that is always
right. It is now clear to me that this kind of parenting mimics the way
they presented being a Jew. You are Jewish. This is what you do to be
a good Jew, and that's it!—no questions, no debate, no nothing! This
has really struck me even as I sit here and write. I feel sad and feel like
I have been cheated in some ways. So many of my stressors and hard
times in life could have been different had I known Jesus and who He
really is. So here I sit, and I guess I can say at this point, "Hi, Jesus,
I'm Heidi, and I'm so glad to know you and feel blessed that I get to
call you my Lord and Savior."

Around early October, I found out that another preschool was
in need of a teacher for their pre-K class, which was exactly what I
had been teaching prior to my resignation. A wonderful mom of a
student I had taught had recommended me to the director of the
school and called to tell me all about the position. I contacted the
school and immediately set up an interview. I can remember vividly
sitting at the head of the table with the director, some teachers, and
two parent representatives. Talking about teaching was something
I was so passionate about, and I just spoke from my heart. I was

honest about how things came to a close at my last position, and I also shared how heartbroken I was. They all could see how much my heart was in it, and the interview came to a close. They told me they would be in touch.

Maybe a day or so after the interview, I received a call from the director offering me the job. I had a really overwhelming feeling about accepting the position. This truly was exactly the position I was hoping for, and it was at a really great school, but I could not shake the feeling in my gut that I had. I've always believed that my gut was a good indicator for me, and it was holding true in this situation too. Now that I was a little more mature in my faith, I brought it to God. I actually had a conversation with Him that went something like this: "Father, I pray that You will convict my heart and guide me in my decision regarding this pre-K position. I'm feeling as though this is not the time for me, but I do not understand why I am feeling this way since this is exactly the kind of position I had held in the past. You tell us not to operate on feelings as we can perceive those feelings incorrectly. I pray, Father, that You will make Your presence known and share Your truths with me so that I know what direction to take."

What a great concept it was talking to God. Who knew that that was all that praying was! For the longest time, I was convinced that I didn't know how to pray. I thought you had to pray using words and scripture from the Bible, but in actuality, praying really is just having a conversation with God. The secret here is that God already knows your heart, but reaching out to God is our way of growing closer to Him. Fortunately for me, I had read a book called *Talking with God: What to Say When You Don't Know How to Pray* by Adam Weber. He explains the simplicity that goes into praying. He says it is just like talking with a friend, and God is excited to hear from us.

I finally got the answer I needed, and I called the director back and told her that as much as I wanted the position, I felt like the timing may not be right as I wanted to be able to travel to see my son, Chandler, while he studied abroad. And Noah had recently started McQuaid, a private Jesuit school, and I wanted to make myself available for him so that he did not have to take the bus home. I was thinking of every possible reason, and the director was so willing to accommodate me. But in the end, I went with my gut and did not take the position. Once I made that decision, I felt a lot of peace and knew it was time to move on. I think, at this point, God had me right where He wanted me, which was in a place where I was focused on Him.

I told the women at my Bible study that I did not accept the position and was going to continue to be available for our group and grow in the Lord's word. The ladies seemed happy for me that I was able to rely on God in making the decision, and they too said that God has a plan. And as things are revealed, we tend to have a greater understanding as to why things happen the way they do.

Chapter 8

GOD REVEALS WHY

Holidays are always a busy time, and they are especially busy when you have to prepare for two kids to come home from college and prepare one kid to leave for a semester in Prague. Unfortunately for me, I seemed to schedule my yearly gyno appointment in October and realized I had not scheduled my yearly mammogram. So shortly before leaving the gynecologist's office the morning of October 19, 2015, I made the appointment for my mammogram. I scheduled it for December 10 at 9:00 a.m. I never really worried about having a mammogram, for breast cancer did not run in my family. However, I have always been on top of things regarding doctor's appointments. And even though this was a busy time of year, I knew the importance of getting it done. It was a typical mammogram where they squish your breasts in-between two glass plates and then proceed to ask you how you are doing. Let's see, how many people would be great in that position? At any rate, because it was a busy time of year, I told them that I would have to leave and not wait the usual time for them to say the scans were good, and I was all set. I just got myself dressed and headed to Wegmans in Canandaigua, New York for a big grocery shop as now with five people in the house, food was disappearing quickly!

Later that afternoon, I was informed that my mammogram showed something, and they wanted me to redo the x-rays.

Apparently, there appeared to be clusters of calcifications. But because I had implants, they were going to have to send me somewhere else for a follow-up mammogram and ultrasound. I asked them if I should be worried, and of course, they just said that the next mammogram would reveal more. So I scheduled that for December 18 and tried not to worry myself about it because, like I said, no one in my family history had had breast cancer, so I likely had nothing to worry about. December 18 came, and the woman who went over the mammogram x-ray with me told me that she was concerned about there being some abnormal activity because of the way the calcifications were clustered. She said that many women experience calcifications and thickening of breast tissue, but the way they were clustered concerned her; and she felt that I should have a biopsy done of the area. Because we were getting close to the holidays, I felt that getting through those with my family was important, and I would deal with this after the New Year. Our family left for a vacation in Florida, and I tried very hard to put this whole thing aside until we got back.

On January 4, 2016, I went to the Elisabeth Wende Breast Care clinic in Rochester, New York, and I had a biopsy done of my right breast. This was when the memorization of scripture and its importance became very clear. I kept repeating in my head Isaiah 41:10 (NLT), "Don't be afraid, for I am with you. Don't be discouraged, for I am your God. I will strengthen you and help you. I will hold you up with my victorious right hand." I was afraid, and the biopsy hurt so badly. I mean, you are literally lying on a table with a hole in it, and your breast falls through the hole, and they cut out a section of tissue. I thought to myself, *I am scared and alone, and I need to find a way to give myself strength.* The only way I knew how in that moment was to focus on the word of God. I was so glad I had been practicing memorizing that piece of scripture. I'm pretty certain that God pointed that verse out to me as one to memorize because He clearly knew what was to come.

The doctor was super nice, and they tried to make me as comfortable as possible. Once the procedure was done, I got myself dressed, and I actually remember driving to the nail salon to treat myself to getting my nails done. My breast at this point was still numb, and so I wasn't in any pain as of yet. Evening came, and the bruising and pain started to appear. I literally looked like someone beat up my boob. I never knew bruising could be so colorful. I can't remember how long after the biopsy, but it was maybe a day or so, and I got a phone call from the doctor stating that I had LCIS, otherwise known as lobular carcinoma in situ. In English, what that means is that I will develop breast cancer at some point in my lifetime but that this was not cancer itself. I thought to myself, *Are you kidding me? So now what?* I had to find a surgeon who dealt with this kind of thing and fortunately got a referral from a friend who had used this surgeon when she had breast cancer. This was a lot to process, and I remember being in my husband Todd's office and speaking on the phone to the doctor who performed the biopsy. She explained the findings and the seriousness of their nature to Todd and me. From there, I made an appointment right away with the surgeon, not really having wrapped my head around what he was going to tell me. All this time, I tried very hard to focus on the verses that deal with anxiety like the following scriptures:

> Don't worry about anything; instead, pray about everything. Tell God what you need, and thank him for all he has done. (Philippians 4:6 NLT)

> Give all your worries and cares to God, for he cares about you. (1 Peter 5:7 NLT)

> So don't worry about tomorrow, for tomorrow will bring its own worries. Today's trouble is enough for today. (Matthew 6:34 NLT)

> When doubts filled my mind, your comfort gave me renewed hope and cheer. (Psalm 94:19 NLT)

> This is my command—be strong and cou-
> rageous! Do not be afraid or discouraged. For
> the Lord your God is with you wherever you go.
> (Joshua 1:9 NLT)

There are so many verses in the Bible that deal with human
emotions. Again, going back to the idea of living in the world and
not of it, we are confronted with so many things that cause so many
emotions of anxiety, sadness, fear, anger, and worry to name a few.
However, when we live of the world, we tend to focus on the event or
situation and play that around in our head. We also complain to people about it as that is our nature as humans. We just go around and
around with the same issue; and all the while, God is there, waiting
for us to bring it to Him. God understood that we would experience
so much in this world that He sent Jesus who lived amongst us. As
much as Jesus encouraged us to have relationships with those around
us, he also reminded us that we should live in a way that pleases God,
not the people in the world.

> And do not be conformed to this world, but
> be transformed by the renewing of your mind,
> so that you may prove what the will of God is,
> that which is good and acceptable and perfect.
> (Romans 12:2)

When we live of the world, we begin to take the advice of others, and our emotions are then dictated by what we hear. However,
when we place our sights on what we can't see and choose to trust
in Jesus, we can begin to direct our sights on the promises made by
God. As we do that, we are transformed in our thoughts, and with
that comes change in our behaviors and attitudes. Again, we can
choose to live of the world or in the world. I now understand that I
can live in this world and really connect with my heavenly Father and
the Holy Spirit and make the choice to do so.

The day arrived when Todd and I would meet with the surgeon.
I had prepared some questions but really was at the mercy of what

the doctor was going to tell me. Fortunately, he was a wonderful man who showed concern and compassion. He listened and gently shared what he needed to. He and his nurse took a ton of time with Todd and me. However, there were not many options for him to offer, and the doctor proceeded to go over what they were. First, I could do nothing and monitor between MRI's and mammograms every six months, or I could do a preventative double mastectomy. I remember first thinking, *That's it? Those are my only options?* But quickly, I began thinking that I would just do the double mastectomy because there was no way I was going to live out the rest of my life worrying if today's test would reveal the inevitable. However, I had a lot to consider. Again, the only thing I could do now was to rely on God and prayer. Fortunately, I had my ladies' group, and they were my prayer warriors. I also had a loving husband who supported whatever decision I felt was best for me. However, when you are in this position, you always want to know what someone else would do; and my husband said that if it was him, he would probably just monitor the situation.

My next step in this process was an MRI, which was scheduled for January 8, 2016. The thought here was to determine that there was no breast cancer. And since the biopsy would only remove a small section, the MRI would reveal more. Again, it was a waiting game, and I kept reminding myself of God's promise to be there to strengthen me and keep me from becoming discouraged. I did my absolute best to stay positive and to just do what they told me to do until I had to make the actual decision as to how I was going to move forward. I remember a conversation we had with the nurse at the surgeon's office, and she really tried to stress to Todd and me that this was a very serious thing and that not moving forward with a double mastectomy was risky because it was so important to catch breast cancer early.

I had some big decisions ahead of me, but at this point, I was leaning toward double mastectomy. However, I knew this would be a big surgery, and I had so much going on in my life. Emma, my daughter, was in Alabama attending Auburn University, and she had just shared publicly that she was a lesbian. Chandler, my son, was getting ready to study abroad in Prague, and this just seemed to really be interfering with my ability to be truly present for both of them, not to mention Noah, my youngest son, who was new to the school he was attending and needed me as well. According to what I was learning about faith in God, they say that you tend to grow the most when you are facing a trial, and I for sure was.

Because of all that I was going through, I knew that this would be an ideal time to help my children to see my faith in action. In September of 2015, interestingly enough, I bought myself a spiral bound notebook, and I wrote on the cover, "A Book of Lessons for My Children." I had ironically started the book for my children, journaling and writing about lessons that come from God. I began the book with a premonition that my life might be cut short, and I wanted my children to have something from me that would show them how to handle situations using your faith and God's word. I had this calling and needed to help my children understand that I wouldn't always be around to teach them or provide answers to them in times of need. But if they grew in their faith, they would learn to be able to use God in those moments and rely on Him for answers. I decided this journal or book would be something they would have so that when I wasn't here, they would have me speaking through my written words. You see, as parents like my parents and others, we try to do the best we can with our children. The one area I felt I fell short in was teaching my children about God. Because I was learning what it meant to have a relationship with Him, it was hard for me to have helped them in their early years. However, by keeping this journal/book of lessons, I felt that through my experiences and using God to help me through them, I could write about them in my journal, and this would help my children see how when we seek God, we gain so much in our lives. We gain peace, love, faith, healing, strength, hope, joy, forgiveness, trust, wisdom, and most importantly, the Holy Spirit. Again, I began this journal prior to my even knowing I was going to be confronted with this LCIS, but this was a perfect time for me to show my children how to use God in those moments of uncertainty and worry. I felt that if I could demonstrate my strength to them, they might begin to see the benefit of finding God and getting to know Him in their lives. This was what I realized Jesus was for. He walked the walk of what God the Father wants us all to live our lives like. He accepted everyone, was kind to everyone, never judged anyone, and provided us with a way to grow closer to our heavenly Father. He was pure and sinless. As humans, we learn that being sinless is only something God can be. And Jesus was God, just in human form. Jesus's lessons on how to be a good person and how through Him we can grow closer to God was something I really wanted my children to understand. I also wanted them to understand that it requires discipline and practice. I wanted to show my children how to use scripture in their lives, for meditating on it and praying it back to God is how we grow close to Him. Jesus walked the walk, and His death was for us. He was the ultimate sacrifice and offering for God. The ultimate sacrifice would help people to live a more honest life. Those who believed in Jesus would grow closer to God and have eternal life. We all continue to sin. But as a believer in Christ, we recognize that we can repent our sins. And when we do, God gives us grace. If we put our trust in Jesus and live our lives closely to how He modeled living for us, then God would be glorified.

So I began that journal entry. I explained in the entry what was happening with my health and shared how it set fear and worry in me. It also made me angry. However, I also shared with them how all of what was going on caused me to turn to God. I shared how I am an anxious person by nature and how it's easy to spend more time dwelling on all the negatives because that is where Satan does his work. He knows when we are weak, and he likes to prey on us in our weakest moments to help turn you against God. He wants to make you believe that God is out there, trying to teach you a lesson or punishing you for being you. I went on to share my lesson of not trying to wriggle away from God's grip, for He cares about our battles especially when they illuminate our weaknesses. He wants us to be thankful for our weaknesses, for they are the very place where His strength will display itself.

Consider it pure joy, my brothers, whenever
you face trials of many kinds, because you know

that the testing of your faith develops perseverance. Perseverance must finish its work so that
you may be mature and complete, not lacking in
anything. (James 1:2–4)

For my children to see me in a trial and see how I was dealing
with it using God was important if I was going to get my children to
see how having God in my life changed me.

A week or so after my MRI, I got the results, and they did
not show any evidence of there being any breast cancer. I was quite
relieved but still knew I was far from being in the clear. After much
prayer and conversation with my husband, I decided to schedule the
double mastectomy. The surgery was scheduled for Friday, May 13,
2016. Now I know what you are thinking, why would anyone schedule a surgery on Friday the thirteenth? However, that was my sister's
birthday, and she was actually born on Friday the thirteenth, so I
felt good about the day. Call me superstitious; but at this point, any
hopeful thinking was a good thing!

From this point forward, life was full of doctor's appointments
as I needed to find out about the whole reconstruction part of this
surgery. However, I was also still trying to be a mom and wife. I
had to get my son ready to travel to Prague and help my daughter
through some tough things, so my mind was preoccupied with mom
things, which in turn helped me not dwell on what was to come.
I'm not going to lie, I think I googled every site that talked about
LCIS; and at this point, I felt blessed that they did not consider this
to actually be cancer. (However, let me note that since the time I was
diagnosed, they have changed that fact. According to my oncologist,
today they do consider LCIS to be cancer.)

It is said that when you become more mature in your walk
with Christ, you can feel the Holy Spirit and conviction on things.
Journaling was such a release for me. Writing about lessons from
God was such a stress reliever for me and the perfect opportunity for
me to show my children how to be strong in the Lord and truly trust
Him. When I look back at the book for them, I really never showed
any emotional outbreaks. I really prayed for strength and upheld

God's promises to help continue to trust that God was in control. Was I afraid? Of course I was! I'd be lying if I said I wasn't. But I also felt a sense of peace, knowing that I had people praying for me, and I had God in control of the whole thing.

My lessons to my children were honest. I shared about days not feeling like turning to God. The days when I made excuses and convinced myself that I didn't have time to focus on God, I shared those moments too and how forcing yourself in those moments to set your sights on God can really change things. I shared something I learned in Leviticus 6. God talked about a flame that burns morning, noon, and night. The flame was to remain lit by people bringing offerings to God, not as a form of sacrifice but as a way of reminding ourselves of the important presence of God in our daily lives. As long as we welcome God into our lives, the flame will always be provided. The flame in Leviticus 9 came out of the presence of the Lord. But the flame that was brought to our lives was through Jesus Christ, His death, and resurrection. When we trust Jesus to be our sacrifice, the Holy Spirit comes to live in us as the blue piercing flame of the perpetual presence of God. God forgives us for not fanning the flame and recognizes that as much as we want to keep our word and follow His instructions, we are not able nor capable. For these reasons, He sacrificed His only Son so that the flame would remain glowing. As long as we recognize the works of Jesus daily, we will be filled with the Holy Spirit and the forever fanning of the perpetual flame.

Keeping busy—getting Chandler off for his semester in Prague, and dealing with Emma's issues of thinking she should transfer colleges—definitely was a blessing because it consumed me with things other than what I was really facing, which was the unknown. So I got Chandler off to Prague safely, and I began to help Emma sort out what to do about possibly transferring to another college where her major would be directly related to her long-term goal. Little by little, time went by until May 13 finally arrived. I have mentioned that I shared a lot of what was going on with my Bible study, my children and husband, my in-laws, my sister, my brother, and my father. However, I made it very clear to my dad that I did not want him to share any of what was going on with my mother. I did this for a few reasons. My mother *never* called me or asked to speak to me when I was on the phone with my dad. Therefore, I did not want the only reason for my mom to call me to be because she felt sorry for me. In addition, my mom has multiple sclerosis, and her health was not good. And stress could complicate her MS in ways that could make it worse. However, not having a mother to turn to with something like this was really hard; I'm not going to lie. I sort of felt bitter about it in some respects but just kept relying on God to walk me through my tough times. At this point, I was feeling His presence and the strength that one can only get through with faith and trust in the Lord.

The morning of the surgery was like any other. Fortunately, Emma was home from college, and so I knew I could count on her to help with Noah and little things around the house, including feeding and taking care of the dog. Todd and I joked before the surgery, like any I may have had before; and I really had no idea how intense this surgery was going to be, and I did not give much thought into how it was going to transform my body. I merely knew that I was at peace with my decision because I would rather play it safe if these clusters meant I was going to get cancer than wait for it to arrive.

My doctor came in and told Todd that he would take good care of me, and then that was pretty much the last thing I remember. I made it up to a room after recovery, and I recall being in excruciating pain. I had drains coming out of both sides of me, and apparently one was not draining well. This little glitch meant that the doctor on call had to manually press on my chest to get the area to drain. And when I tell you the worst pain ever, I tell you no lie. Because of this little setback, I had to stay a second night in the hospital. After finally being discharged, I arrived home to countless meals being brought by wonderful friends; and my kids and husband really catered to my every need. The moment I was able to shower was a scary time. I knew, at that moment, I was going to see a disfigured image in the mirror, and I asked God at that moment to help me see myself as whole. The bruising, the stitches, the pieces of skin, they were really something to take in. However, God enabled me to be strong, and I don't think I even cried. I believe my greatest fear lied in Todd seeing me. I thought to myself, *Will he be able to get past this and see the woman he loves?* I think many women must go through that scary moment of revealing themselves to their husband. It's kind of funny when you think about it because love begins sometimes in the physical realm of attraction; but after years of being together, it certainly grows into much more. And that is for sure why I think my husband was able to see beyond what I was seeing. The healing process was long as I was still having problems with my drains, but it was amazing to feel surrounded by so much love from friends. I had friends taking me to doctor appointments, bringing meals, and my Bible study group came to my family room to have our weekly gathering. My new best friend during this process of healing was my recliner. But little by little, things improved, and the removal of the drains was the absolute best!

It had been about nine days since the surgery, and my surgeon said he would likely call Sunday night with the results. Mind you, I had already had a biopsy and an MRI, so I didn't really give any thought to the results of the breast tissue pathology. In my mind, I did not have breast cancer, I just elected to have the surgery so that I would not get breast cancer in the future. Emma, Noah, Todd, and I were sitting around the island in the kitchen when the phone rang at 7:00 p.m. It was my surgeon. So I left the kitchen and went into the office so that I could hear him better. I remember sitting down and him saying, "So I have the pathology results from the mastectomy, and they found a small malignant tumor in your right breast." People always say that when you hear something like that, you don't hear anything else after those words; and that was so true. I didn't know what to ask, what to say, or even how to listen. I did manage to ask one question: So what now? He said that I would need to have another surgery to remove lymph nodes to see if the cancer had spread because they had not taken any in the first surgery because we were not aware that I had cancer. He assured me that the tumor was very small and that, as far as stages of cancer, it was stage 1 because we caught it so early. He said the nurse would be in touch with me to schedule the next surgery, and that was it. In a matter of moments, my world changed; and I remember walking back into the kitchen and breaking down in Todd's arms. I couldn't believe that I had breast cancer. It seemed so surreal. I remember just feeling overwhelmed and a feeling of complete shock. I also had a small sense of relief, for if I had not opted to have a double mastectomy, my life could be completely different. I really do not remember a lot from that time on other than really feeling like I needed to delve into my prayers, and my Bible-study ladies were amazing during this time. I really owe so much to them as they helped me to stay strong and focused on the Lord, which sometimes is hard to do when you are dealt some scary things in life. Life sort of just went on from this point. I had hair appointments as usual, I spent time with friends and I had one special visit with a friend who gave me an Alex and Ani bracelet that represented transformation, faith, and resilience. I honestly can't think of anything more representative of this time in my life, and I was so touched to have received such a thoughtful and beautiful gift. It really meant the world to me at the time and continues to mean a lot to me. At any rate, life just moved on; and I was blessed to have the friends I did at the time. I remember long walks with my friend; and those times with her meant the world to me. I could cry with her and really let down my guard and just be scared in the moment. What I know for sure is that although we can gain strength in the Lord, we still can be emotional and cry too. I went to college orientation with Emma, registered Noah and myself for the hunting course, celebrated Noah's birthday, had Father's Day at the lake, and really just lived a normal life. June 24 came, and that was the day of the lymph node surgery. This was going to be the surgery where I knew I would fear the results. This would reveal if the cancer had spread. The other worst part about this timing was that all of my kids would be home at the lake for the Fourth of July, and I knew that my surgeon was going to call on Sunday, July 3 at 7:00 p.m. because that was when he made his calls. Of course, he reassured me to just have fun; but sometimes that is an easier thing to say for the person who is not going through a scary situation.

July 3 was Clam and Jam at Keuka Lake, and we chose to go to the Waterfront where there was going to be live music. Chandler had friends at the lake, and we all cruised over by boat and had Noah drop us off. We call him our Buber as he usually drives the boat when we have had a few drinks. We danced to live music, had some fun cocktails, laughed, and just all had the best time. I knew I had to gather myself before the 7:00 p.m. phone call, and I can remember sitting on the edge of the bed in our bedroom at the lake, waiting for the phone to ring. I also remember saying out loud, "God, I know you are with me at this moment, and I pray that you can give me the strength I will need to deal with whatever comes my way." Just then at 7:00 p.m., the phone rang, and all I heard was, "I have some good news for you!" At that moment, my heart stopped beating out of my chest, and all I remember from that moment on was my doctor saying, "Now go and enjoy your Fourth of July at the lake!" My lymph nodes came back clear, and my cancer did not spread! Praise the Lord! I ran out of the room screaming, and everyone was hugging and just so happy. Friends on our lake road came over, and it was just a wonderful moment I'll never forget. I felt happy that I had had the presence of God in my life at this time because, in my past, I would have been more likely to dwell on things and think of the worst-case scenario. But I felt more positive and that I would take whatever came my way with courage and grace. I was scared but hopeful—I guess you could say. I trusted that God would provide me with what would be needed either way. What an amazing thing for me to have God in my life and a relationship with Him. I'm not sure how I would have gotten through all the waiting without having had the ability to trust. I always tell my children that, in life, we have to walk by faith and not by sight. At that moment, it was so true!

Life returned back to some normalcy as I had my reconstructive surgery, and I felt free to not have to wonder about whether or not I was going to get breast cancer.

I was so grateful to my Bible-study ladies for all their prayers and support.

Chapter 9

KEEPING IT REAL

Reflecting on my spiritual growth at this point reminds me of how much I have matured in my faith. Being able to really use God in a circumstance in my life is so humbling. Before my relationship with God, I would have spiraled into a depression and would have allowed my mind to wallow in the negativity of a situation. I am now aware of how when you set your mind on the truths so eloquently written in the Bible, you are able to change your patterns of thinking. Having a relationship through Christ with our God gives us hope. I was proud of how hard I worked at this and was willing to share it with anyone and everyone—everyone except my parents, my sister, or brother. You see, the one area I have yet to really be able to strengthen myself with the word of God is with them. It is almost like I am two people. When I talk to them, I become the person they see me as; and when I speak to others, I seem to be able to share my experience in a way where others can see the Lord working in me. If you recall, my family had opinions about everything, and you were always supposed to never question anything and go along with their line of thinking.

Something I love so much about my ladies' group and studying the word of God was the way they welcomed my questions. My whole life I have always felt as though any question I asked was a dumb one. Comments were always made after you asked a question that led you to believe you were an idiot for asking it. However, my questions in Bible study always were met with excitement as I helped others to dig deeper. You see, everyone in my study was raised as a Christian. Most of the women knew all the stories, yet I did not; and I was so amazed by them because they excited me. I craved learning more about God and Jesus as I knew the more I learned, the more I would grow in my faith. And that meant so many good things to me. A struggle that I had in reading the Bible was interpreting scripture inaccurately. This was disappointing to me because I wanted so badly to be correct in my thoughts. But in my group, with all of these women, I had confidence. This was new for me because, in most areas of my life, I lacked confidence. However, because I had such a desire to learn, I would ask those "dumb" questions, and the best part was how those questions actually ended up helping others in the group. We were doing a study on the book of John, and in chapter 13, Jesus talked about the meaning of washing the feet of His disciples. I had shared with the group that I thought He was making reference to the baptism and cleansing yourself of sins and giving your life to Christ. However, I was not correct in my interpretation and learned that in this passage, Jesus was making reference to the fact that He was not above others and was displaying the quality of being humble. Even in these ancient times, people were beginning to develop the attitude that they were above others based on what they had; and Jesus demonstrates that we all should be serving to each other—no one being above another. Now I could have left the group feeling stupid or ashamed for getting it all wrong, but these ladies were the best. My questions were always welcomed, and in fact, two women reached out to me later that day, thanking me for my questions for they helped them to dig deeper. For the first time in my life, I feel like my questions and my comments have value. And to be doing that in the word of God is so meaningful for me. Feeling valued for my thinking is something I never experienced before, and it is an amazing feeling. So much good can come from seeking God's truth. I was just so grateful that I had the courage and confidence to do this pretty much on my own. Yes, I did have support from my

Bible-study friends, but it was up to me to take initiative to learn, read, and study scripture.

Growing in your faith is not something that happens overnight. It takes time, practice, commitment, and desire. Without any of those, you are sure to fail. However, God has given us all spiritual gifts, and some of us are fortunate enough to have certain godlike qualities that come naturally. Although my husband was raised a Christian, I have never seen him open a Bible or even pray. However, I was incredibly drawn to him in the early years. And I would say, it had to do a lot with his spirit. Todd is super interested in how the mind works and in fact studied it all through college being a psychology major. Some of us have to make a conscious effort in our everyday lives to do better and be kinder. However, these godlike characteristics are what drew me to Todd.

I was raised in a setting in Long Island where what you had played a role in who you were. Material things were of great importance, and my world was small. I knew Long Island, and that's pretty much it. I can remember saying to Todd one time when he was talking about his summer, "What do you do in Rochester in the summer?" I asked it with a bit of an attitude, like I was so much better than him. Remember, I grew up in Long Island where we all went to summer sleepaway camps or on teen tours cross-country and to Hawaii; and if we were home, we could go to the beach. Rochester is not any place I was familiar with; but I knew one thing, it didn't have an ocean. In my judgmental mind, it must have been a boring place to live. Todd went on to share how he had a cottage on a lake, and they would go tubing, have clambakes, cookouts, and just did a lot of boating activities. Well that peaked my interest as that sounded really fun. The way Todd shared this was so humble. He wasn't trying to prove anything to me or compare his life to mine. He was merely speaking from a place of joy in the way he lived his life. My husband demonstrates this humbleness all of the time. I consider this to be such a Christlike trait and one I've been so blessed to witness. In addition, my children are growing up with such an appreciation for what they have and the willingness to share it with others. Todd never has the attitude that he is better, smarter, more worthy, or above anyone else. This is a quality we all strive to have as Christ demonstrates this in the Bible. I'm just super blessed to have married someone who naturally has this quality.

I'm sharing all of this because as I continue to grow in my faith and strengthen my relationship with God, it is evident to me that I still struggle with things. I wish I could say that my life is perfect, and it is because I study the Bible, go to Bible studies, read devotions, journal, and share the Lord's word any chance I get. However, that would be a complete lie. I am better than I was in who I am, but I have some strongholds that can bring me down. When I say down, I mean way down. This is where I have come to realize, and I will quote Jennie Allen as she says it best in her book *Get Out of Your Head*, "They say authors write books for two reasons: either the author is an expert on the subject, or the subject makes the author desperate enough to spend years finding the answers." I continue to seek God in my life because I believe this will be the only way for me to rid my mind of the strongholds I have. I have learned that people can give advice or say anything to try and impact our emotions. But telling someone not to feel a certain way is not going to really change their way of feeling. Take me for instance. I have been programmed to believe that I am dumb. This is based on years of people telling me that, and I am believing it to be true. There are times when Todd will laugh at something I say, and I become defensive as my knee-jerk reaction is to think he is laughing *at* me. But he says the only reason I think that is because that is how I have been made to think. So how do I change that line of thinking? Todd encourages me to get some counseling. But I believe that with greater effort, I can use the word of God to change it for me. Just as I had to redirect my thoughts when I was worried about my breast cancer, I need to redirect my thoughts in this situation as well. This one is a hard one because when you have been programmed for years to think a certain way, it is so hard to not only think differently but to believe it as well. Since how we feel is directly related to how we think, then I know I need to learn to think differently.

Don't copy the behavior and customs of this
world, but let God transform you into a new per-

son by changing the way we think. Then you will
learn to know God's will for you, which is good
and pleasing and perfect. (Romans 12:2 NIV)

What a powerful message and one I would have missed completely had I gone through life believing that making my matzah
balls makes me a good person. It is interesting because as I sit here
and write, I constantly think about what my family would say to
me if they were reading this. Then I have to talk myself into saying,
Why do I care? Passing judgment on others is something God frowns
upon. Everyone has a history, which shapes who they are and what
they become. I don't hold ill feelings about my family in any way.
I know that we all do the best we can as parents. However, I think
what God has helped me to do is to really look within myself and
recognize things that are good and things that need to be worked on.
We are all human, and we all are sinners.

I think becoming a Christian has really helped me to understand what it truly means to be a better person. And in trying to
do better, you have to face the reality of your imperfections. Let me
say that again, *in order to do better, you have to face the reality of your
imperfections.* Just as some people refuse to go to counseling, I think
some people turn away from God because, in God, you are reminded
of who you really are. Sometimes there are some not so great things
about yourself that you have to come to terms with. Avoiding God
is one way to avoid facing your true self. Reading the beautiful story
of Jesus helps you to recognize that the ultimate goal as a Christian
is to allow the spirit to change you and renew your mind. This is no
easy task, and again, it takes desire, commitment, and effort. In addition, you have to already have some knowledge of who Christ is and
how building a relationship through Him to God is what our desire
should be. There truly is no other way to know God than to know
who He was in human form.

Has anyone ever asked you what you think God looks like?
When I was younger, my image of God was always a figure of a mum-
my-like being. Because God was such a mystery to me, I assumed
you were not supposed to have an image of what He looked like.

In fact, growing up, we were never supposed to write out the word God. When you referred to Him in writing, you would write G-d. However, God is real. And now if asked, I would describe Him just as Jesus is pictured. The best part of this image is He wasn't beautiful so to speak, He didn't wear the best clothes, He didn't associate with the wealthy, and He never judged. I think we can all agree that this is not how society portrays itself today. We place a lot of emphasis on outward appearance and fail to focus on who people are on the inside. I'm guilty of it too. That's our sinful nature, our human side. But Christ is there to remind us that He died for our sins, and we need to do better; and that is why we set our sights on Christ so that we can be reminded of how we should be living our lives.

People should not dictate how we live or how we think. God has illustrated for us how we should live our lives according to all of the examples of truths so beautifully written in the Bible. The trouble is, when you first dabble in faith, reading the Bible seems so overwhelming. I vividly remember going to hotels where there would be a Bible in the drawer, and it always scared me. The pages always were paper thin, and the cover was always a special leather-like material. However, I am here to say that Bibles come in many different fashions, so to speak. I have a Bible that is the NIV (New International Version) on one side and written in The Message on the other. I didn't even know what that meant until attending my first Bible study. My friend Kelly suggested I try a Bible like this because the message is a little easier to understand than some of the older languages the Bible is written in. Right off the bat, I became less intimidated by this once-scary book. I also learned that you can write in your Bible. I have passages that are underlined and notes written in the margins. Another Bible I purchased is a Life Principles Bible. This Bible explains how scripture relates to real life. In the end, once you have a Bible, it is important to understand how to delve into it. I am still in the learning phase of this because this is something I believe you learn overtime, and you get better at it with continued practice.

Seasons are another concept I have had to learn in becoming a Christian. I'm not talking about seasons related to weather but seasons of our lives. There are times in our lives when everything is going smoothly. It is oftentimes in those seasons when we don't engage as much with God. Unfortunately, due to our human nature, we often will cry out to God in the tough moments but forget who He is in the good moments. Thanking God in all situations is something I am learning to practice. There are blessings to be learned in both good and bad times, but you have to look for them. Again, our human nature causes us to see things in a way that gives us what I call tunnel vision. When we are in a trial, and we fail to acknowledge God, we can spiral into a frenzy. But as a Christian, it is important to understand that turning to God and crying out to Him is what He wants; yet He also wants to hear praise in the good moments too. Finding ways to be joyful even in the midst of a crisis is important. For me, I believe that is the true meaning of faith. Being aware of Satan lurking and wanting to take our joy away is equally as important. Satan wants to do everything he can to interrupt our relationship with God. Priscilla Shirer has a wonderful Bible study called "The Armor of God." This armor is our best defense against the negative that roams around us. Satan tries very hard to create doubt in your mind. He wants to open up old wounds because then he has you in a place where you feel anger, hurt, unforgiveness, and you spiral into a place far from God. When you become aware of the things Satan is doing, you are better able to fight off the demons by using the truths from God. The full armor of God involves wearing the belt of truth, the breastplate of righteousness, shoes with the gospel of peace, shield of faith, helmet of salvation, sword of the spirit, and prayer. The devil, as I have learned, targets the areas we are weakest in. Priscilla shares in her Bible study that humans have three distinct parts: our body, which allows us to relate to the physical world; our spirit, which allows us to connect to God; and lastly, our soul. Our soul is what makes us unique. The soul is made up of your mind, your will, your emotion, and your conscience. In simpler terms, it is your thoughts, your ambition, your feelings, and your moral compass (Priscilla Shirer, *The Armor of God*). Some days, I have no problem putting on the pieces of armor; and other days, I can't seem to find them. In Ephesians 6:10–18, God instructs us about how to use our armor and He says it best.

> Finally, be strong in the Lord and in his mighty power. Put on the full armor of God, so that you can take your stand against the devil's schemes. For our struggle is not against flesh and blood, but against the rulers, against the authorities, against the powers of this dark world and against the spiritual forces of evil in the heavenly realms. Therefore, put on the full armor of God, so that when the day of evil comes, you may be able to stand your ground, and after you have done everything, to stand. Stand firm then, with the belt of truth buckled around your waist, with the breastplate of righteousness in place, and with your feet fitted with the readiness that comes from the gospel of peace. In addition to all this, take up the shield of faith, with which you can extinguish all the flaming arrows of the evil one. Take the helmet of salvation and the sword of the Spirit, which is the word of God. And pray in the Spirit on all occasions with all kinds of prayers and requests. With this in mind, be alert and always keep on praying for all the Lord's people.

What a powerful message from God. Because of who we are as humans, our road map can steer us in the wrong direction; and this can lead us to dangerous territory. But we are all sinners, and faith is how we receive righteousness. Our belief in Christ is how we honor God as He was the ultimate sacrifice. No more animals had to be brought to the altar. God just wants us to recognize who Christ is and, in doing so, make an effort to draw closer to Him through His Son. It is through our acceptance of Christ that we are able to have peace from God. God acts as an anchor in our lives as the circumstances of our world are constantly changing. This is why I practice my faith. I need something to anchor me because my thoughts can get out of control; and with that comes worry and anxiety. I get angry with myself for choosing to feel this way because I can choose to focus on God. This is the perfect time for me to remember to put on my shoes of peace and walk with God and, in those moments, pray, trust, and be grateful. It sounds so simple when I'm writing, but it takes a lot of practice and habit to be able to walk this walk.

Chapter 10

LEARNING TO PRAY

I was having lunch one day with my husband's cousin, and she was not in the best place, so to speak. She and I have always really connected at a deeper level. She is able to be real with me, and I am able to be real with her. While at lunch, I guess the things I was sharing came from a place that could only have been from God. She said that she recognized a certain peace in me, and we got to talking about how I was seeking God so I could grow in my faith. We talked about prayer a lot. If you recall, earlier in my book, I mentioned being at holiday dinners where Todd's aunt, would pray over the food. So I asked her, "How do you not know how to pray? You were raised Christian, and your mom seemed to know how to pray. So how do you not know how to do that?" This was an eye-opening thing for me to learn. My assumption was that all Christians knew how to pray. For me, praying as a Jew was always prayers over wine, *challah* (bread), or some other Hebrew prayer over candles. But learning to pray was going to be a big part of growing in my faith. In addition, learning that it didn't involve fancy language or any type of rote wording was really eye opening to me. Prayer did not have to include scripture either.

Although growing up, I didn't enjoy reading. I think it was because I never found what really interested me. However, I love to read books about how faith works in your life. I guess you can say they are spiritual self-help books. One time, as I mentioned earlier, I came upon a book titled *Talking with God: What to Say When You Don't Know How to Pray* by Adam Weber. If you have not read this book, I highly recommend it as he answers the questions many of us have about praying, like "What should I pray about?" "What exactly do I say?" "Are there things you shouldn't say?" "Do you need to speak out loud?" And lastly, "Where do you even begin?" I am pretty certain Todd's cousin never really shared her concerns about not knowing how to pray. Many people don't because, as an adult, this is something you should know how to do by now. However, I know, growing up Jewish, I never really prayed to God. Like I said, I prayed over wine, bread, and candles. They were prayers in Hebrew and rote in the language we used. Learning to pray was going to become an important step in growing my faith. I dove into this book ready to learn. What I learned is that praying is very simple. It seems awkward at first because we usually don't talk out loud unless we have a physical being we are talking to. But when you talk to God, He is only there in the spiritual sense, so it seems a little strange at first. Adam begins the book pretty similarly to my experience with Todd's cousin. He met a person from his congregation, and the conversation led to the question of how to pray. I love what Adam said in his book: "'When you pray,' Jesus said, 'don't do it to be seen. Don't do it to impress others, like hypocrites often do.' They might sound impressive, but they actually have it all wrong. Yup, they've missed the boat. Prayers do not need to be long, there's no need to use big words. God isn't impressed with how we pray or the things we say. In fact, he already knows what we need, even before we start" (Adam Weber).

I loved the way Adam explained his experiences of growing up and reciting prayers around food and before sleep. He also speaks to how the words were always the same. I could relate to this and how this was similar to my Jewish upbringing, but I was about to learn something that has forever changed my life and my relationship with God. Through this book, I learned to just talk. I began praying in the shower as I felt like no one could hear me there. I would just tell God that I wanted to develop a relationship with Him so that I could enter into a new spiritual life. I wanted to live not according to rules and laws but according to the spirit. And with that, I told Him I longed to find His peace and love that I know I could find through my acceptance of Jesus Christ as my Savior. If God could give Jesus life after death, I knew He could renew my life in a way that would be fulfilling and filled with loving, healthy relationships, something I so longed to have in my life; and I was finally about to open the door so that I could have healthy relationships with my husband, my kids, and others close to me.

It's interesting when you have a preconceived picture of what praying looks like, and you then learn that the image you had is all wrong. Praying does not have to be a somber thing. You can laugh with God, cry with God, and share any emotion you feel in the moment; for God created us, and these emotions come from Him. It may seem silly to think of someone praying in the shower, but God doesn't care where you pray. As long as you are coming to Him, He will be there to listen.

This brings me to a very important thing I learned. For as much as we pray to God, we need to be still and listen to His voice. This is something that requires understanding in the way God speaks. I read a wonderful book called *Whisper: How to Hear the Voice of God* by Mark Batterson. I spoke of seasons earlier, and one season I recently went through was not hearing God's voice. I was going to my Bible study regularly on Tuesday mornings. Well let me correct that. As I write, we are currently in the midst of the COVID pandemic, so I was actually zooming on Tuesday mornings. We had recently completed a few different studies on Revelations, First, and Second Samuel, and we were getting ready to do a study on Psalms. We were studying from the same author; and for whatever reason, I just was not feeling as though God was speaking to me even though I was in His word. When I first started to read Scripture, I was told that I would hear God, and the scripture would speak to me. Early in my journey, friends would tell me to just open my Bible to whatever page and read, and God's message would be revealed in some way based on what I read. The idea is that God will present you with what you need to hear in the moment you need to hear it. Sometimes that works, but other times, I did not find that this was happening.

Frustration would set in, and I would turn away altogether, which in the moment, I should have recognized that it was Satan trying to pull me away from having a relationship with the Lord. One of my friends in our Bible study suggested I read the book *Whisper*, and I'm so glad I did. Reading and gaining perspective on being a Chrisitan and walking with God is so important. As I have repeated over and over, it takes commitment, desire, and practice. You do not wake up one day and say I want a relationship with God. You pray about it, and then it is there. There is no app that gives you that immediate connection. The connection one has from God depends on *you* and how much *you* are willing to put in the work to develop that relationship. I was willing, and so I delved into this book, hoping to find my way back to God. This is when I found out that there are seven love languages God uses to speak to us. They are scripture, desires, doors, dreams, people, promptings, and pain (Mark Batterson). The thing one needs to understand is that when we want to hear from God, we need to listen with our eyes and our hearts, as well as our ears. But most importantly, you have to have the Spirit in order to discern God's voice. If you have not accepted the Spirit into your life, it is easy to say all the signs or messages are just hogwash. However, whenever you hear a message or see a sign of how God is prompting you in some way, you can always cross-check that message with scripture.

I have a few instances where I can say I clearly heard God's voice prompting me to do things. The first big moment for me was when I was offered the preschool position that was what would have been the perfect job. I remember asking God if this was going to be the right decision for me, and the only peace I felt at that time was when I made the decision not to accept it. Mark Batterson shares the importance of going through five tests when trying to discern the voice of God. One of the tests is what he calls the peace test. When peace surpasses understanding, you know in your heart of hearts that you are making the right decision. I had that peace, and I was glad I heard and felt it because shortly after that decision, I was confronted with breast cancer.

Another instance when I felt God leading me was during one of my mornings at Bible study. We, as a group, welcomed new members to join at any time. We wanted to make people feel welcomed, and so we could be in the middle of a study, and someone would join the group. At the end of our two hours, we would open up the study to prayer requests. During this particular morning, a woman fairly new to the group asked for us to pray for her daughter who was feeling persecuted by other students at school because of her strong Christian beliefs. She went on to say that her daughter wanted to start a Bible club, and another student mocked her by saying how they would like to go to her club and see why they hate gays. Well my ears perked up at that moment as my daughter is gay, and this is a sensitive topic for me. Another group member began saying that she was sorry as she knows there are members who have gay people in their lives, but she went on to share how her daughter is vehemently against gay marriage; and from that moment on, my mind was in another place. I was very upset and met with my prayer partner who could see I was visibly upset, and she tried to console me with the understanding that the gay issue is one that is a huge factor in churches, and many disagree on the issue. I told her that early on, when I became involved in the ladies' group Bible study, it was hard for me because that was about the same time my daughter was coming out as a gay person. It hurts me to this day to think that my daughter was afraid to share her identity with me because she knew I was trying to grow in my Christian faith, and she thought I wouldn't love and accept her. That hurts to hear as Jesus was known to love and accept all the people, even those who may have been viewed as outcasts in society. To think that my daughter would think that being a Christian would make me judge her is sad. At any rate, my prayer partner suggested that I pray about what happened and see where God would lead me. Sure enough, I did just that and prayed that God would direct me on how to handle my feelings about comments made in the group; and with that, I happened to come upon Matthew 18 where we are instructed to share our hurts with fellow Christians when we have felt hurt by them. There it was—God's way of speaking to me. I immediately got out a pen and paper, and I began to compose a seven-page letter to the member in my group and mailed the letter, thinking this could be the end of a friendship. I spoke from a place in my heart and used what I was hearing from God to express my thoughts. When I reread my letter, I thought to myself, *How did those words come from me?* I felt I wrote it so eloquently, and I truly believe God had His hand in all of it. A few days later, my phone rang, and I saw my friend's name pop up. I took a deep breath and answered the phone, preparing myself for what was to come. Much to my surprise, my friend thanked me for the letter. She went on to apologize and how it made her realize that she needed to be careful with her words and that this was a weakness of hers. In the end, no one left feeling a sense of hurt, but both of us walked away stronger in our faith and our friendship. Good job, God!

Another instance where I used prayer was a big one was when my sister and I planned a trip to Florida so that we could celebrate my dad's eighty-fifth birthday with him. It would be a quick trip, but I was happy to do it and glad my sister was going to be there with me. Shortly before we were leaving, my sister informed me that she would not be joining me because something came up at work, and she needed to be present in New York for it. I can remember the feeling of my heart sinking into my stomach. Recently my dad and I had a huge disagreement, and this was weighing on me as my sister was on my side so that if it came up, I knew my sister would be there to support me. This was where faith was so important. I needed to trust God in this moment and understand that, in all things, God has a plan. So I did what I learned to do best in these moments; and with a lot of encouragement from my ladies' group, I began to pray and asked them to cover me in prayer as well. Proverbs 3:5–6 was what I prayed on. Something I learned from my friend Kelly is that when you find a piece of scripture that speaks to you, you can use that scripture and pray it back to God. Proverbs 3:5–6 says, "Trust in the Lord with all thine heart; and lean not unto thine own understanding. In all thy ways acknowledge him, and he shall direct thy paths." So I began to pray, "Father, I want so badly to trust You in this situation. I want to believe that there is a reason You are sending me to Florida on my own. I pray that You will walk with me and guide me on this path. I trust that You have bigger plans for this visit, and I pray that Your goodness is revealed." Off to Florida I went, and I changed my visit so that I flew in one day, spent the night, and flew out the next evening.

My mom, as I mentioned, has multiple sclerosis, and she was in bad shape, both mentally and physically. She was receiving OT at the time, and her OT recommended that she talk with a counselor and go on some medication for her depression and anxiety. My mother is quite strong-willed, and she "knows everything." She has this mindset that she is always right and will discount what anyone else says if it doesn't align with her thoughts. My father asked that I try talking to my mom as I had many times in the past. Sadly, my mom would sit in a room in the front of their Florida home with the blinds closed by herself all day. Even while I was there, my dad, brother, and I would be in the family room, and my mom would not join us. If you wanted to visit with my mom, you had to go to the dark front room. I went to the room and began talking. I spoke a lot about her choosing not to have joy in her life. I went on to say that she could be so much happier if she went on medication and got her mental health in a better place. She told me she didn't like drugs, and I asked her why and got no answer. I asked her if she was happy, and she said *no*! I asked her if she was enjoying anything about life, and she said *no*! I asked her if it was normal for someone to sit by themself all day, talk to no one, go to bed, and do it all over again the next day. I shared how she would feel better on the drugs, and she might be able to experience some joy. At this time, I wasn't feeling as though I had made a whole lot of progress, but she did choose to go out to eat with us, which was huge because she usually wouldn't leave the house unless it was for her hair appointment. A reminder here that a lot is going on behind the scenes as I had broken down to my Bible study the Tuesday before I left because I was so worried about what this visit would be like by myself. All my friends had me covered in prayer. The next day, Sunday, the routine with my mom began at 5:45 a.m. She sat at the kitchen table that was set up for her the day before at 4:00 p.m. with all her makeup and a mirror, and she put on her face, so to speak, and then got dressed and got on her scooter so she can make her way into what I refer to as the cave. Now remember, my mom had not seen me in over a year, and she wheeled right by the family room to go sit by herself—normal or not normal? This was what I had to endure most of the weekend, but I did make many attempts to sit with her in the cave. Finally, it was close to the time when I was going to leave for the airport, and I heard my mom call for me. I headed for the room, and my mom asked me a question, and literally, this feeling of confidence came over me. The words just flew out my lips. I started speaking about how everyone's life was not all wonderful, and hers was not the only one terrible. I wanted her to see that everyone faces trials in their lives, but we have to choose how we face those trials. I said to her, "You think my life may be perfect and wonderful, but it is not." I told her that I had never planned on sharing this, but I felt now was an appropriate time. I said that in 2016, I got diagnosed with breast cancer and had to undergo a double mastectomy. Her posture, which was usually slumped, suddenly changed as she sat more upright engaged in what I was sharing. I told her that I was not telling her for any other reason than for her to understand that we all face hardships in life, but that we have to choose how we will (1) face the hardship, and (2) live our lives after it. I told her that I chose joy and that I began working on my faith, and my belief in God helped strengthen me. My mom was focused on her guilt about not knowing (again all about her), but I told her not to feel guilty as that was not the reason I was sharing this now. I explained how I had a wonderful support system in place, and my family and friends were so instrumental in helping me deal with it all. I told her that if she felt really badly and wanted to do something, she could make me a promise that she would try the antidepressant. With some hesitation, she finally agreed. At that moment, my dad walked into the room and said, "Heidi, I never heard you talk like this." At that moment, I knew the words were coming from the Holy Spirit. Two lessons were learned here: First is in life, you have choices on how you face trials. You can allow that trial to dictate your life, or you can choose to find joy so that you can live happily. The second is that you need to pray. Through prayer, you have an opportunity to seek God and place your trust in Him. This is hard because sometimes prayers are not answered immediately, or they are answered in a way that doesn't match our thinking. But living your life trusting God will help make your life so much easier and fulfilling. It is hard, and it is also challenging at times, but the alternative is allowing the world and things around you to dictate your life and who you are and how you think. We *all* get caught up in this, and it is very damaging to your soul. When you find time each day to seek God and just talk to Him with no fancy words and not always asking for something, you learn something very valuable. First, this is an important step in growing in your faith and relationship with the Lord, and the best part is He is always available to listen. And when you take the time to be still, you just might hear back from Him.

Chapter 11

Breaking a Cycle
and Recognizing
Purpose

I have spent countless hours of my life trying to figure out what my purpose in life is. I was a good teacher and felt that was my calling, yet I would soon learn God had other plans. After leaving the preschool position years ago, I had signed up on a jobsite called Indeed. I would periodically receive alerts on available teaching jobs and come across one for teaching preschool at a Christian school. I thought to myself, *What the heck, I'll just send my résumé and see what happens.* Literally, a few short hours later, I received a call with interest in setting up an interview. As my gut had led me in a lot of decisions, I truly thought to myself, *I will go with this because, if it is meant to be, it will be.* Fast-forwarding, I ended up getting an offer for the kindergarten position, and I accepted. I spent the entire summer on the internet, seeking fun lessons, and working on my classroom. I was excited and thought that this would really resonate with me because I would be teaching again, and I would be in a school with Christian values. It was going to be perfect—my identity, *teacher*! I truly thought that this was going to be perfect other than I would be going from zero to one hundred as I had not worked full-time in so many years. My youngest son, Noah, was not super excited about it as it was his final year of high school, and he liked coming home to me being there and with good home-cooked dinners. Todd supported my decision as he always supports what makes me happy.

As I mentioned earlier, I have read a lot of books that are spiritually based, self-help kind of books. One such book was *Your Beautiful Purpose: Discovering and Enjoying what God Can Do Through You* by Susie Larson. One part in her book, which resonates with me, is that sometimes God inspires us to do something. However, when this something takes up all our time and consumes us, we may essentially miss our calling. I believe I missed mine, thinking this job was it. However, I quickly learned how wrong I was as I wasn't taking the time with God daily, my family was eating rotisserie chickens and store-bought meals, and I was very unhappy in the position. So many factors did not align how I had thought they would, and so I resigned from the job long before the year had ended as the stress was taking a toll on me and, in turn, my family and my relationship with the Lord.

Early on, as I attended my Bible study, I remember telling the group, after grieving my preschool teaching position, that I now realized that God had me exactly where He wanted me. He created me to be a mother and a disciple to my children of His word. At the time, I felt very confident in that role and excited by it as I thought I would be really good at it and was proud to be in a position to be able to do this. But as life would have it, the world around me had me questioning, "Was this it?" As we know, strongholds can really play a factor in our lives, and the best way to fight them is with the word of Jesus. We need to remember that some of our thoughts cannot possibly come from God because of His character. That is the important point in developing a relationship with Him through Jesus. My inability at times to accept that where God has me as a mother, wife, and home-maker is where he wants me. I may see other women with careers and families, and I think, *Why can't I do that?* However, when I go to God with this stronghold, I am reminded of what he says about jealousy, which I guess, you can say, is the problem here. The feeling like I was never enough or good enough lives within me. But I know that is not what God thinks of me. However, not having had this relationship with God early on and having parents who made you feel like you were not enough can really wreak havoc on your psyche. Having the feeling of jealousy of others does not come from God.

> For jealousy and selfishness are not God's kind of wisdom. Such things are earthly, unspiritual, and demonic. For wherever there is jealousy and selfish ambition, there you will find disorder and evil of every kind. (James 3:15–16 NLT)

However, as I have devoted more time to writing, so much has been revealed to me. Our faith is about an intimate relationship with God. And as we follow Him, we will recognize things about ourselves that may not be clear otherwise.

It is easy to move through life and just do what has been done before, so to speak. What I mean by that is you only know what you know based on how you were raised. I grew up not hearing the words *God, faith, love,* and *prayer*. However, for whatever reason, I have broken the cycle and have put those words at the forefront of who I am and how I raise my children. I never end a conversation with my children without an *I love you*, and I always encourage them with God's truths from the bible. I can recall multiple times sending scriptures to my children as words of encouragement just as I can recall them asking for me to send them scriptures.

Recently, my youngest son, Noah, was preparing to take his test to earn his private pilot's license. He was extremely stressed out as he had not had a lot of flight time in the plane he was taking his test in. Now anyone who knows Noah knows that stress is not a word really in his vocabulary. He is one of the most super laid-back people I have ever met. However, this test was really riding on him; and so he sought my wisdom. I could sense just how much he needed something to calm him down. My words would only go so far because I could only validate his feelings. But I took some time to find some meditation podcasts, meditation music, and even threw in something on Spotify called Your Daily Prayer. I told him to listen to them when he was going to bed at night. When I asked him if he gave the music a try, assuming that was what he would choose to listen to, he actually told me that he liked the prayer ones better. Ahh, that was music to my ears. I know my children look to me to guide them in the word of God. I sort of think my children and my husband both do. When we have large family dinners, I am called upon to say the prayer. Years early in my desire to seek God, I vividly remember the first time I prayed out loud. My children had never prayed with me or heard me pray out loud, and I remember them all trying to hold in their laughter. My reaction initially was feeling upset, but I understood that this was new to them, and even mature Christians find praying to be awkward at times. Years later, my prayer at Thanksgiving brought my children to tears. God was present. And at that moment, I knew God's plan and purpose for my life; and that plan is really starting to come to life for me. I'm grateful. Thank you, Jesus, for renewing my spirit and equipping me with this gift that I can pass on to my family. To know my children know they are loved and to hear how much they appreciate me is what brings me so much joy and makes me realize that my purpose—although not what I would have thought it would be—surely is one I value, for the cycle has been broken, and my children have been given the gift of what it means to believe in God and to lean on Him. Modeling for them the importance of prayer and seeking God is a priceless gift and one that I have worked so hard to give them. For this, I am so grateful that I had the confidence to go out on a limb and explore who Jesus is.

> But blessed is the one who trusts in the Lord, whose confidence is in him. They will be like a tree planted by the water that sends out its roots by the stream. It does not fear when heat comes; its leaves are always green. It has no worries in a year of drought and fails to bear fruit. (Jeremiah 17:7–8)

I have really felt God's blessing here, and I can freely say that I am not captive to my childhood; for my confidence in the Lord is what causes me to move forward and continue to seek and grow in my faith. Although this is not something my parents might be proud of—for I likely have continued to disappoint them—I am confident in being a child of God and glad I heard His voice so that I could walk with a purpose each day. My wealth comes from raising three amazing children who continue to amaze me with their kindness, thoughtfulness, love, desire to achieve their dreams, and their respect for God and the role they are learning He plays in their lives. It also comes from having a husband who provides for us so we have a blessed life; and I am able to stay home to love him and my children so that when they walk in the door at the end of the day, they can feel a sense of calm and know a hot home-cooked meal is on its way. All of the stars aligned, so to speak. But truly, I know this was God's plan from the beginning.

> For we are God's masterpiece. He has created us anew in Christ Jesus, so we can do the good things he planned for us long ago. (Ephesians 2:10 NLT)

Chapter 12

WE ALL HAVE GIFTS

When I first set out on my journey, I did so because I was so lost and felt as though, without my role as a teacher, I was nothing. It was what gave me an identity, but it was a false identity because there was so much more to who I am. This continues to be revealed in so many ways. But had I not had the confidence in the Lord, these gifts would have gone unnoticed.

> God saved you by his grace when you believed. And you can't take credit for this, it is a gift from God. Salvation is not a reward for the good things we have done, so none of us can boast about it. (Ephesians 2:8–9 NLT)

Becoming aware of just who God is has enabled me to look within and see just what my gifts are. That in and of itself is one of the greatest gifts imaginable. I have learned that you do not earn your way into heaven or work your way, but it is merely a gift to you for believing in Him.

Growing up, I saw the value in doing nice things for others with the idea that you would be rewarded for that. The truth is, that is not the truth. God created us all with special gifts that touch people and help create a path for your life. The idea is that when we use our gifts in a way that is pleasing to God, we receive His ultimate gift, which is our eternal life in heaven.

I am God's work in progress. And the more I commit to learning who Jesus is and the role He had on earth, the more I believe I am on the right path. Isaiah 66:9 speaks of how brokenness brings forth faith. When we seek God in those broken moments, we are brought closer to Him. Beth Moore, at a conference I attended, made reference to how the mystery of God's gifts are wrapped and sometimes hidden in mystery so that the presentation is even sweeter. Our passions can sometimes be born out of pain, and it is this brokenness that brings forth faith.

I try to remind myself to use these beautiful gifts that were made clear to me through my faith.

Chapter 13

Having Hope

It can be so easy to lose sight of good when so much bad is happening. However, without trials and hard times, people will not call out to God. It can be in those trials that you learn the most beautiful things, but you need to look for them. It is important to recognize that not all of God's gifts are given to us freely. Sometimes it is only when we ask Him to point them out to us that we are able to visibly see what would have been easily missed.

I think it is clear to say that my resignation from the preschool job could have looked like the world coming to an end, so to speak. However, it was because of that event in my life that I came to the ladies' group years ago. When we are going through a rough time, it is really hard to have hope and see the blessing. But hope is what you get when you believe in Jesus.

Death is always a tough one when people ask me about how you explain having hope when someone close to you dies. In the early years of me seeking God, I came across Rick Warren who is a pastor at Saddleback Church in California. His "Daily Hope" is something I subscribe to as the message is usually very relatable and always in tune with scripture. Rick lost his son to suicide. And months after his son's death, he gave one interview on CNN to Piers Morgan. He was asked whether he ever doubted God or His existence. His response has been one I will always remember. He said, "No, I never did, but

I doubted His wisdom." He went on to explain. "My kids have never doubted that they had a father and that I loved them but that they have often doubted my wisdom and maybe that I made the wrong decision." Rick Warren also explained how he never questioned his faith in God, but he questioned His plan, reiterating that there was a big difference. He went on to explain how God is a good God and a loving God. He was certain that God was not to blame for Matthew's death as his son took his own life by choice. God permits things to happen because He gives us the freedom of choice. If you choose to do wrong, then you can't blame God. His belief is that even through despair, there is always hope, and we are never to give up (pastors. com) (Religion.blogs.cnn.com).

The blessing in this devastating event was that both Rick and his wife, Kay, were able to bring to light the importance of mental illness to the church. As a result of the Warrens openly speaking about it, many people began to feel they could open up about it and seek help. He and his wife said they were devastated by their son's suicide, but they were not destroyed. They committed to the idea that they were going to choose joy as "we're not in control, but we do have greater hope, and we do have a source of joy that isn't based on circumstances" (pastors.com). That is such a powerful statement and one we often lose sight of because it challenges our faith, which in turn gives us hope. And having hope can bring us joy. I once read this quote that happiness depends on what happened, but joy does not.

> Satisfy us in the morning with your unfailing love, that we may sing for joy and be glad all our days. (Psalm 90:14)

> But the fruit of the Spirit is love, joy, peace, forbearance, kindness, goodness, faithfulness, gentleness and self-control. Against such things there is no law. (Galatians 5:22–23)

Sometimes the whys in life go unanswered; but if we are to continue on a journey of faith, we need to be okay without knowing the why. Trusting God is one of the hardest parts about being faithful. God sees things from a different perspective, and that is an important thing to understand as a Christian.

> For my thoughts are not your thoughts, nei-
> ther are your ways my ways...as the heavens are
> higher than the earth, so are my ways higher than
> your ways and my thoughts than your thoughts.
> (Isaiah 55:8–9)

God doesn't think like us and knows more than we know. When we lean into the promises of God, we can begin to see how He thinks, and this is what helps us grow in our relationship with Him and, in turn, have trust and hope.

> But he said to me, "My grace is sufficient for
> you, for my power is made perfect in weakness."
> Therefore I will boast all the more gladly about
> my weaknesses, so that Christ's power may rest
> on me. That is why, for Christ's sake, I delight in
> weaknesses, in insults, in hardships, in persecu-
> tions, in difficulties, for when I am weak, then I
> am strong. (2 Corinthians 12:9–10)

When we have hope in the Lord, joy can sneak up on us as long as we view the hardest lessons as gifts from God. Our joy flows from a grateful heart, so it is important to sometimes thank God for your challenges because they give us a greater opportunity to see Him at work.

Chapter 14

THERE IS A REASON

Some stories don't really have endings, and I believe this to be one of them. We all have choices in life in how we handle what comes at us. I continue to hold on to God's promises to keep me centered, but I would be lying if I said I don't go to places of sadness in how I have been viewed by my family. It is a daily battle in my mind to set the thoughts aside that can consume me about who my family sees me as. I know I am God's child first, and I'm grateful that I found God in my life and know that He is proud of me for seeking and for leaning on His truths. But the painful reminders of who my family sees me as will be a battle that I will be fighting until the end. However, I am going to choose to be grateful for this situation because had I not been in this situation, I may never have sought out who God is, and I may never have had a relationship with Jesus Christ. It's not easy to find that amidst the hurt sometimes, but I know that is the truth. My focus needs to be beyond the hurt, and I need to embrace the fact that my identity is in Jesus, not in who I've been made out to be by my family.

The constant reminders challenge me daily, and I'm grateful that I can cry out to God and grateful for my husband and my children who see me in a totally different light. This month, for my children, has been a very exciting one. We began by celebrating my youngest son's accomplishment of earning his private pilot's license.

Next came my daughter's promotion to agent and the fact that in the forty years her company has been in business, she is the youngest person at twenty-three to become an agent, And lastly, my son Chandler worked hard to land himself a new job in Nashville. These are what you call proud-mama moments. I am proud of my children for setting goals and achieving them. These are the kinds of things you want to share with your family because they are moments that deserve celebration. Just yesterday, I did just that. I called my father to tell him about the great news about Chandler getting this new job and having an opportunity to move to Nashville. In sharing that news, I went on to say how happy I am for all my children, and I am so proud of them. My father's reply was, "Heidi, they have you beat." I didn't know what he meant by that, so I asked. And his reply was, "they are making more money than you." I don't choose to measure things by dollars and cents, so this comment was hurtful. You would expect the reaction to be something of, "Heidi, you have raised three wonderful children, and you have been a wonderful mother to them." But as much as I long to be complimented by my family for something, I need to come to terms with the fact that God has me here for a reason. Had I not been in this situation with my family, I may still be trying to be a good person because I made my matzah ball soup. How sad that would have been. I reached out to my friend Kim, and her reply to my dad's response was, "I'm sorry. That is not the response you deserve. Little does he know, you're about to become a best-selling author. And the irony is that it's because of him!—or despite him." This really resonated with me, not because I think I am or ever will be a best-selling author but because of my situation. I have been able to seek wisdom from God and share my story so that others who may be in a similar situation may be able to learn the importance of having a relationship with Jesus, and in learning, they too may want to share the good news of the gospel. Sometimes it is really important to see God's purpose beyond the pain just as Paul did when he spoke to the Philippians. He proclaims the notion that his imprisonment helped him to proclaim the gospel. I believe his message in Philippians 27–30 (MSG) really aligns with my story.

> Meanwhile, live in such a way that you are a credit to the Message of Christ. Let nothing in your conduct hang on whether I come or not. Your conduct must be the same whether I show up to see things for myself or hear of it from a distance. Stand united, singular in vision, contending for people's trust in the Message, the good news, not flinching or dodging in the slightest before the opposition. Your courage and unity will show them what they're up against: defeat for them, victory for you—and both because of God. There's far more to this life than trusting in Christ. There's also suffering for him. And the suffering is as much a gift as the trusting.

I began my story with the intention of reaching someone who may be in a place of faithlessness; however, I can also say that my story is really a story about recognizing how you can turn pain into joy, for serving our God is something I'm honored to be able to do.

Chapter 15

FREE

I thought my book was coming to a close, but God had another plan. I would like to end this story by sharing what it means to feel free for the first time in my life. Sometimes in our lives, we feel imprisoned by people, and we get sucked into the belief that we can't get out. Life is about choices. And when we feel like we are behind bars, we need to remind ourselves that those bars exist because we allow thoughts to control us. We are free to leave on either side, but sometimes we fear what that freedom will bring, and so we remain in prison because sometimes the familiar can seem more comfortable.

Having faith and following Christ so that I could have a relationship with God involved taking a risk many years ago. However, I chose to remain under the control of thoughts that held me captive my entire life. A recent event in my life has caused me to take another risk so that I can freely worship God and be the person He created me to be. I have decided to walk out of prison, so to speak. I have chosen to free myself by distancing myself from those who see me as someone I am not—those who seem to think that I am dumb, selfish, unkind, unthoughtful, and the list goes on. Something inside of me has gained the strength that can only come from God so that I can walk out of this prison and seek the joy and peace I long for in my life. I have finally come to the place where I don't believe those lies I've been told my whole life. Sometimes it takes me writing a letter and then reading the letter to help me see what's true and what is not. I wrote this letter to a family member, but I do not plan on sending it. The letter was a way for me to share what this prison cell has been like for me. It also was a way for me to recognize that we can believe lies when we fail to listen to the voice of truth, which only comes from God. I think the best way to sum up how I choose to live my life is through the words of a song by Matthew West called "Family Tree." The song is about changing your family tree because yesterday is not something that has to define you. By placing your faith in God, the chains that once bound you no longer will; and as a result of this, God's dream for your life is revealed. By trusting in God, you will find love and change the course of your life for generations to come. I am God's child, and He chose me and calls me loved and promises to restore what is broken. And with that, I will bring new life to *my family tree* because I choose God, love, and something better for me and my family. God has opened the eyes of my heart. And although I love matzah, I don't need to believe that cooking matzah balls is what will make me a good person. I am free—finally free!

Father, I am grateful for the life you have given me. Regardless of all of the ups and downs in life, I recognize how, through a relationship with Christ, I am able to use Your words and truths to help navigate my life. It is a daily challenge but one I will continue to work hard on as I know the glory it brings to You and the peace it brings to me. My hope is that my story may touch one person who will choose to see the importance of having a relationship with You. Thank You for blessing me with life and for challenging me daily so that I can turn to You and Your word. In Jesus's name, I pray. Amen.

∞

About the Author

Heidi Clarke is a wife and a mother to three children. She has always had a love of writing, and enjoys learning, about how to strengthen her relationship with God. Her greatest desire is to help her children learn how to seek God in their own lives so that they too can develop a relationship with him. She spends her summers on Keuka Lake with family and friends; and in the winter, she enjoys the peace found at her farmhouse.

CPSIA information can be obtained
at www.ICGtesting.com
Printed in the USA
LVHW021817080622
720759LV00004B/563